The Rockwool Foundation Research Unit
Study Paper No. 22

Source Country Differences in
Test Score Gaps: Evidence from Denmark

Beatrice Schindler Rangvid

University Press of Southern Denmark
Odense 2008

Source Country Differences in Test Score Gaps: Evidence from Denmark

Study Paper No. 22

Published by:

© The Rockwool Foundation Research Unit and University Press of Southern Denmark

Copying from this book is permitted only within institutions that have agreements with CopyDan, and only in accordance with the limitations laid down in the agreement

Address:

The Rockwool Foundation Research Unit
Sejroegade 11
DK-2100 Copenhagen Oe

Telephone	+45 39 17 38 32
Fax	+45 39 20 52 19
E-mail	forskningsenheden@rff.dk
Home page	www.rff.dk

ISBN	978-87-90199-17-3
ISSN	0908-3979

November 2008

Print run:	300
Printed by	Special-Trykkeriet Viborg a-s

Price:	65.00 DKK, including 25% VAT

Foreword

In 2004 the Rockwool Foundation decided to launch a research project that would focus upon the relationship of young immigrants to the Danish educational system, including an investigation of the attitudes of these young people towards education and of the benefits that they obtained from attending primary and lower secondary school (i.e. the obligatory stages of schooling) in Denmark. It has been evident for a number of years that non-Western immigrants do not make much use of the Danish educational system, and that far too many of those who do go to Danish educational institutions fail to complete their courses. If this educational pattern of non-achievement is not broken, then it will greatly hinder the true integration of immigrants from non-Western backgrounds into the Danish labour market, and consequently into Danish society.

In order to determine the learning outcomes for young immigrants from their attendance at Danish primary and lower secondary school, the Rockwool Foundation Research Unit contacted the Danish PISA Consortium to arrange a special PISA survey. The results of this survey were presented in a book published in 2007 by the University Press of Southern Denmark entitled *PISA Etnisk 2005* (PISA Ethnic 2005), edited by Niels Egelund and myself. This special PISA survey made possible in-depth analyses of school-pupils' performance, including the performance of pupils from non-Western backgrounds.

The study presented in this paper makes further use of the very rich PISA dataset from Denmark to investigate the significance for the PISA scores of the countries of origin of the participating school pupils. In addition, the paper presents a series of results related to the PISA participants' expectations with regard to their future employment and family lives.

At the same time as this paper is published, a book in Danish is being published by Gyldendal which presents an overview of the entire Research Unit project on the relationship of young non-Western immigrants to the Danish educational system. This book is entitled *Indvandrerne og det danske uddannelsessystem* (Immigrants and the Danish educational system), ed. Torben Tranæs.

I would like to take this opportunity of thanking Beatrice Schindler Rangvid, AKF, the Danish Institute of Governmental Research, for her contribution to the project and to Astrid Würtz Rasmussen, Helena Skyt Nielsen and Leif Husted for commenting on Rangvid's paper. I also offer my warmest thanks to the staff of the Rockwool Foundation and their Board of Directors, to Tom Kähler, the Chairman of the Board, and to Elin Schmidt, Managing Director of the Foundation, for their cooperation on this project. As always, the work on the project has been carried out in complete academic independence from the Rockwool Foundation; however, without the financial resources that the Foundation has made available, the project would not have been possible.

Copenhagen, November 2008   *Torben Tranæs*

Contents

Abstract		7
1.	Introduction	9
2.	Literature review and determinants of immigrants' educational achievement gap	11
3.	A brief overview of immigration in Denmark	13
4.	Empirical approach and data description	15
4.1.	Empirical approach	15
4.2.	Data and sample	17
	Dependent variable	18
	Variables of interest	20
	Explanatory variables	20
5.	Estimation results	25
5.1.	Full sample results	25
5.2.	Subsample results	28
6.	Why do immigrants with similar socio-economic background underperform compared to Danes?	35
6.1.	Do immigrants attend different (and worse) schools?	35
6.2.	Difference in attitudes and expectations	36
	Estimation Results	41
6.3.	Additional possible factors behind the gap	45
	Ethnic capital in the source country	46
	Ethnic capital among compatriots in Denmark	47
	Family formation	49
7.	Conclusion	51
Appendix		53
References		55
Publications in English from the Rockwool Foundation Research Unit		59
The Rockwool Foundation Research Unit on the Internet		62

Source Country Differences in Test Score Gaps: Evidence from Denmark

Beatrice Schindler Rangvid[1]

Abstract

As a novel feature in PISA research, we are able to analyze source country differences in student performance. We combine data from three studies for Denmark in the PISA 2000 framework to investigate differences in the native-immigrant test score gap by country of origin. In addition to the controls available from PISA data sources, we use student level data on home background and individual migration histories linked from administrative registers. We find that both raw and SES-adjusted native-immigrant reading test score gaps vary considerably across source countries. While adjusted gaps are large even in the second generation for students originating from Lebanon, former Yugoslavia and Turkey, second generation students from Pakistan do much better. Students from former Yugoslavia and Pakistan who use Danish as the main family-language do not perform significantly worse than otherwise similar native Danes. Girls from Pakistan also perform at similar levels to native Danish girls with similar SES backgrounds. Analyses including school fixed effects show that differences between schools help to explain the remaining gaps, as do differences in expectations and attitudes towards family and working life.

---

[1] AKF, Danish Institute of Governmental Research, Nyropsgade 37, DK-1602 Copenhagen V, Denmark. Phone: (45) 4333 3400 , fax: (45) 4333 3401, and e-mail: bs@akf.dk.

1. Introduction

Immigration is going to strongly impact the future of education in Denmark, as immigrants and particularly children of immigrants increasingly account for a larger proportion of school-age children. This development highlights the need to better understand the educational attainment of immigrants. Existing research has provided evidence on important differences by country (or region) of origin for educational attainment, for the school-to-work transition and for the integration of immigrants into the labour market (Nielsen et al. 2003, Cortes 2004, Riphahn 2003, Bauer & Riphahn 2007, Van Ours & Veenman 2003), but in the field of school achievement in European/Western societies, few such analyses have been undertaken due to data limitations. However, in order to design effective policies for integration of immigrants, it is essential to know which groups are particularly exposed to the risk of under-achievement and at what stages of the educational career these gaps arise.

As a novel feature in the second wave of the international PISA study of 2003, a range of participating countries chose to ask students to state in which country they were born. However, the resulting information available in the international PISA is not very helpful for quantitative analysis, due partly to high non-response rates, and partly to inadequate immigrant sample sizes. For the special case of Denmark, however, we can cope with these challenges better: first, we can link information from administrative registers on country of origin[2] (COO) to the PISA dataset and thereby substantially increase the number of students with valid information on country of origin; and second, we can increase the size of the sample of immigrant students by combining data from three Danish student assessments using the PISA 2000 set-up (one is the Danish subsample of the international PISA 2000 study; the other two are replicate studies using the PISA 2000 framework). The combination of data from three PISA assessment studies yields a dataset which includes information on about 2,000 immigrant students (and 7,500 native students).

This study expands on the existing literature specifically through its analysis of PISA test scores by source country. We begin the analysis with descriptive statistics on the test score gap relative to native Danes by country of origin. Then we investigate whether the gaps can be explained by student characteristics, starting with a simple regression on the means (OLS), and then continuing to consider possible heterogeneous effects along the test score distribution by quantile regression methods. We also allow gaps to differ by a range of student characteristics such as gender, immigrant generation, parental education, etc. In a second step of the analysis, we investigate further possible explanations of the test score gaps that remain after accounting for differences in student

---

[2] Throughout this study, we use the terms *source country* and *country of origin* (COO) interchangeably.

socioeconomic background. First, we estimate regressions including school fixed effects to explore whether differences between schools account for part of the gaps. Next, we consider whether differences in attitudes and expectations related to family and working life are associated with the test score gaps. Finally, we suggest some additional factors that might be related to the gaps such as the levels of ethnic capital both from the home country and among compatriots in Denmark, and factors related to family formation. However, we do not present an empirical assessment of the importance of these factors, since they are available at the country level only, and cannot therefore be readily embedded in our empirical analysis.

We aim at answering the following questions:

1. Do the test score gaps relative to native Danes differ by country of origin, and can students' own backgrounds explain these test score gaps?

2. Do gaps and their sources differ by immigrant generation, language used at home, gender, or parental education?

3. Can differences between schools attended by Danes and immigrants from different COOs explain the remaining gap?

4. Are differences in attitudes and expectations related to family formation and working life related to test-score gaps?

This paper is organised as follows. The next section briefly presents the related literature and discusses potential determinants of educational achievement gaps. Section 3 provides a brief description of the recent immigration to Denmark. The data and some descriptive statistics are presented in section 4. Results from the empirical analysis are reported in section 5. The last section is the conclusion.

2. Literature review and determinants of immigrants' educational achievement gap

The native-immigrant gap for outcomes such as wages, educational attainment and achievement is well-documented for many countries. Entorf & Minoiu (2005) and Schnepf (2007) examine the gap for (PISA) test scores, and Chiswick & DebBurman (2004) for years of schooling. Nielsen et al. (2003) analyse the school-to-work transition, and Adsera & Chiswick (2007) and Chiswick, Le & Miller (2006) present results for the native-immigrant wage gap. These studies document the fact that immigrants (as a group) achieve less favourable outcomes than natives.

Several studies also document substantial performance differences across countries or regions of origin; see for example Bauer & Riphahn (2007), Riphahn (2003), Van Ours & Veenman (2003), Jakobsen & Smith (2003), Kristen & Granato (2007) on educational attainment gaps, and Cortes (2004) and Rooth & Ekberg (2003) for results for wage and unemployment gaps. These studies document considerable heterogeneity in outcomes for immigrants from different source countries, even when differences in socioeconomic backgrounds are taken into account.

We are aware of only two studies reporting results for country of origin – most studies use regions of origin. Riphahn (2003) examines the probability of attending the highest-track school in Germany (Gymnasium) and length of completed education. She finds that the lowest probabilities for children's advanced school attendance are measured for young people from Italy, Turkey, and former Yugoslavia, and the largest gap in completed degrees are found for Turkey at the very bottom and then Italy, Spain, former Yugoslavia, Portugal, and Greece. However, the composition of the immigrant population in Riphahn (2003) differs markedly from ours, since Turkey and former Yugoslavia are the only non-Western countries for which country of origin effects are estimated[3], the other countries of origin considered in Riphahn's study all being Western countries[4]. Van Ours & Veenman (2003) find for second generation immigrants in the Netherlands that, conditional on the education of their parents, most immigrant groups have an educational attainment level that is similar to that of native Dutch young people. Only for first-generation immigrants from Turkey and Morocco do they find that even conditional on the educational level of their parents these groups have a lower level of educational attainment than native Dutch people. Thus, their main conclusion is that the observed lower educational attainment of second-generation immigrants can be explained by their parents' lower average level of education.

---

[3] Western countries are defined as EU-25, North America, Australia and New Zealand. All remaining countries are defined as non-Western countries.
[4] In Denmark, student samples from these countries are of negligible size.

The present study expands on the existing literature specifically through its analysis of PISA test scores by country of origin. In addition, the research also examines whether gaps differ across subgroups of the immigrant population delineated by immigrant generation, language used at home, gender and parental education. Furthermore, this is the first study to consider factors related to family and working life as possible explanations for the gap.

3. A brief overview of immigration in Denmark

Historically, Denmark has never been a country that attracted substantial numbers of immigrants. Until the mid-1980s, only 3% of the population were immigrants, and 60% of these originated from Western countries. Since then, the number of Western immigrants has remained almost unchanged, while the number immigrants from non-Western countries has increased sixfold. Thus today 9% of the population are first or second generation immigrants, and 75% of these have origins in non-Western countries.

The most recent chapter of the immigration history of Denmark begins around 1970, when immigration mainly consisted of 'guest workers' from Turkey, Morocco, the former Yugoslavia and Pakistan, whereas earlier immigrant cohorts had consisted almost exclusively of immigrants from the developed countries, especially the other Nordic countries (Sweden, Norway, Finland and Iceland) and Germany.

After the first oil crisis in 1973, the immigration pattern changed and, as in many other European countries, the immigration of 'guest workers' stopped, while refugee immigration grew considerably, especially after the mid 1980s (Pedersen, 1999)[5]. Thus, some immigrant groups have had a longer migration history in Denmark and are mostly second generation immigrants (e.g., descendants from economic migrants from Turkey and Pakistan; Figure 3, section 4.2), while others are dominated by more recent arrivals (e.g. refugees from Somalia, Iraq and Afghanistan). Immigrants from the former Yugoslavian republics have come in two waves: the first wave arrived as guest-workers some decades ago, while the second wave are war refugees, mostly from Bosnia-Herzegovina, who came to Denmark at the beginning of the 1990s.

---

[5] Nevertheless, the immigrant flow from the guest-workers' countries of origin continues, driven by marriage migration.

4. Empirical approach and data description

4.1. Empirical approach

We start the analysis by presenting descriptive statistics of test scores for subsamples of natives and immigrants. Then we apply multivariate regressions to control for inter-group differences in estimating native-immigrant test score gaps by country of origin.

To address the first research question, i.e. whether there is a reading score gap for the different country of origin populations, we regress the continuous reading score variable (READ) on a set of country of origin fixed effects (CooFE). Next, we control for student and family characteristics (X) such as student's gender, family structure and number of siblings, parental education, occupation, cultural and social communication, cultural possessions, home educational resources and the number of books in the home to examine whether lower educational achievement among immigrants from different countries can be explained by these factors. If i indexes individuals, the baseline model for the pooled sample is:

$$READ_i = \alpha + \beta_0 CooFE_i + \beta_1 X_i + \varepsilon_i \qquad (1)$$

Where the α, β_0 and β_1 are coefficients and ε_i is a random error. The β_0 coefficients provide information about the association between country of origin and reading scores, and thus – with Danes being the reference category – the β_0 coefficients are the estimates of the native-immigrant test score gaps for the respective countries of origin. If immigrants from a specific country of origin lag behind natives in their educational achievement, the β_0 coefficient for that country yields a negative and significant estimate. If this difference is due to compositional effects of socio-demographic characteristics of the student and his family, the effect should disappear once the control variables (X) are introduced. Note that we do not include immigrant-specific variables such as 'years since migration' (for the parents), language spoken in the home and immigrant generation in the regression on the pooled native-immigrant sample, since they are either not defined or are constant for native Danes. Instead, we present subsample results in section 5.2 and we show results for the 'immigrants-only' sample including these variables as controls (also in section 5.2.).

The baseline specification (1) estimates coefficients at the mean of the conditional test score distribution. While estimating the size of the test score gaps at the mean is useful, it is quite possible that the gaps differ across the test score distribution. For example, we would like to know whether the bottom of the distribution differs systematically from the top. In order to extend the analysis to the entire test score distribution, we present quantile regression results. By construction, quantile regressions estimate the test score gaps relative to natives at an arbitrary point on the conditional test score distribution. For the θth quantile, a common way to write the model (see for example Buchinsky, 1998) is

$$Quant_\theta(READ_i|CooFE_i, X_i) = \alpha + \beta_{0_\theta} CooFE_i + \beta_{1_\theta} X_i \qquad \theta \in (0,1) \qquad (2)$$

where $Quant_\theta(READ_i|CooFE_i, X_i)$ denotes the θth quantile of $READ_i$, conditional on the regressor vectors $CooFE_i$ and X_i. The important feature of this framework is that the marginal effects of the covariates, in particular of the country of origin indicators (given by β_{0_θ}), may differ over quantiles. If the β_0 coefficients differ over the quantiles, this is evidence that the gap relative to natives for students from a given county of origin is not constant along the conditional test score distribution. Thus, by supplementing the estimation of the conditional mean functions with the estimation of the conditional quantile functions, we expect to get a more complete picture of the pattern of test score gaps.

The baseline specification (1) also restricts estimates to being equal across subsamples. Therefore, in the next step of the analysis, we estimate equation (1) separately for different subsamples of students[6]. We divide the immigrant sample along various lines: by immigrant generation, language spoken at home, parental education and gender. We then pool each subsample with the native sample and estimate equation (1). For example, we compare results for the pooled sample of natives and first generation immigrants to results of a regression on the pooled native and second generation sample. A comparison of the $\beta_0 s$ from each pair of regressions shows whether the second generation has reduced its gap relative to natives compared to their first generation compatriots.

Moreover, as mentioned above, immigrant-specific covariates cannot be meaningfully included in regression samples together with native Danes. However, in a subsample regression for immigrants only, we can analyse the impact on child's test scores of immigrant-specific variables ($IMspec_i$) such as language spoken at home (Danish or other), years since arrival for parents, and immigrant generation. This regression can be written as:

$$READ_i = \alpha + \beta_0 CooFE_i + \beta_1 X_i + \gamma IMspec_i + \varepsilon_i \qquad (3)$$

In the last part of the empirical analysis, we look for additional explanatory factors that might be responsible for the remaining test score gap. First,

---

[6] We would have liked to present results for the heterogeneity of the estimates of socio-economic background variables across countries of origin, too. However, probably due to the small sample sizes, the results were hardly significant and showed no systematic patterns. We therefore do not present these results in this paper.

including school fixed effects ($SchoolFE_i$), we investigate whether differences across schools attended by Danes and immigrants account for part of the gap. Second, we examine whether differences in attitudes and expectations (AE_i) towards education, work and family life are related to the test score gap relative to Danes. We estimate the following equations:

$$READ_i = \alpha + \beta_0 CooFE_i + \beta_1 X_i + \lambda SchoolFE_i + \varepsilon_i \qquad (4)$$

$$READ_i = \alpha + \beta_0 CooFE_i + \beta_1 X_i + \lambda SchoolFE_i + \sigma AE_i + \varepsilon_i \qquad (5)$$

Some of the control variables, in particular the school fixed effects and attitudes and expectations are probably not exogenous to educational achievement. As such, the results should be seen as associations rather than clear causal relationships. All equations, except equation (2), are estimated by Ordinary Least Squares methods and the standard errors are corrected for clustering at the school level.

4.2. Data and sample

At the core of this study are data from three PISA assessments for Denmark. All three assessments use the framework of the first PISA wave (2000), with reading being the main assessment area. We use only reading literacy test scores as measured in the PISA framework as our outcome measure, because the maths and science tests were given to half of the students in the sample only. Since the cell sizes are small for several countries of origin in the reading test score sample already, using maths and science scores would result in very small country of origin subsamples. The first of the three PISA studies used is a Danish PISA replicate study conducted in 2005 sampling students in schools with high immigrant concentrations (PISA Ethnic). The second assessment focuses on Copenhagen schools and was administered to all 9th graders in Copenhagen public schools and a number of private schools in 2004 (PISA Copenhagen). The last part is the Danish subsample of the international PISA 2000 assessment (PISA 2000). Table A1 presents selected summary statistics for each of these datasets[7]. As is seen in the table, the subsample of the international PISA 2000 study, which is drawn to mirror the entire population composition in Denmark, has a much lower immigrant share, 5%, than both the Copenhagen sample and the PISA Ethnic dataset (27% and 31%), which sample students at schools with high immigrant shares.

The composite variables of cultural and social communication, cultural possessions and home educational resources have not been provided for the

---

[7] These datasets contain observations with valid information on the key variables, namely source country and reading scores. In both the PISA Copenhagen and the PISA Ethnic datasets we lose a number of observations due to the non-reporting of civil registration numbers by school heads, which means that register information cannot be linked to the PISA data.

PISA Copenhagen data. Instead, for this dataset, we include the single items that enter into the calculation of the composites in the regressions, and we include missing value flags to indicate the differential use of these variables across datasets. The index of occupational status (HISEI) is not available in the PISA Ethnic dataset. Instead, we have information from the administrative registers on issues covered by the HISEI index, such as parental occupation, years of work experience, and household income. Thus, while we use HISEI for the PISA 2000 and the PISA Copenhagen dataset, we use the register information for PISA Ethnic data and use missing value flags in a similar manner as above. We have chosen not to include age as a control variable, since the student's age when attending 9th grade is probably more of an outcome than an input in the education production function.

The combined dataset includes 1,892 immigrant and 7,511 Danish students. We define immigrant students as students born to parents from non-Western countries. Immigrants with (at least) one native Danish parent are defined as native Danes. Immigrants from Western countries are very few in number and are excluded from the analysis[8]. In our final dataset, we include separate indicators for ten source countries (those with more than 50 student observations in our combined sample). These countries are: Turkey, former Yugoslavia, Pakistan, Lebanon, Iraq, Morocco, Somalia, Vietnam, Iran and Afghanistan. Immigrants from other non-Western countries are grouped into a residual category. All observations are included in all regressions, but we have chosen to report results for the four largest countries of origin only (those with more than 150 observations) due to the very small samples for the remaining countries.

Dependent variable

The PISA tests focus on the demonstration of knowledge and skills in a form that is relevant to everyday life challenges rather than how well students master a specific school curriculum. Using Item Response Theory to compute the scores, PISA maps reading performance on a scale which has been standardized to an OECD average score of 500 points and a standard deviation of 100 points. Figure 1 shows kernel density estimates for reading scores by country of origin. The shapes of the densities for students from Lebanon, Turkey and former Yugoslavia is similar to that of Danish students, but shifted to the left (indicating lower test scores, overall). The test score distribution for Pakistan is flatter, suggesting a greater spread of performance levels.

---

[8] In Rangvid (2007) it is shown that students with one immigrant and one Danish parent and immigrant students from Western countries perform at similar levels in the PISA test to native Danes.

Empirical approach and data description 19

Figure 1. Kernel density estimates for reading scores by COO.

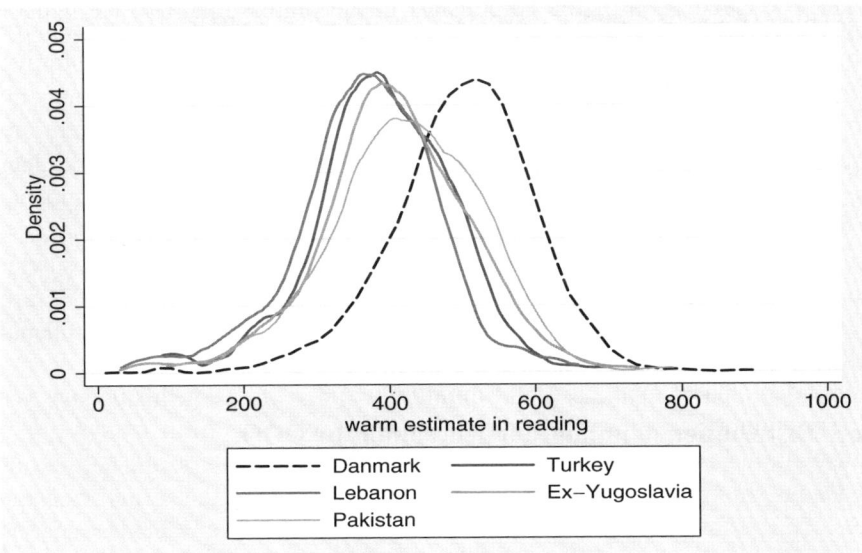

Figure 2 shows the means of the test score distributions by country of origin. For three out of four source countries, the gap relative to Danes is close to or even larger than one standard deviation (SD=100) of the reading test score distribution. For Pakistan, the gap is smaller, but at 3/4 SD still substantial.

Figure 2. Test score distribution by COO.

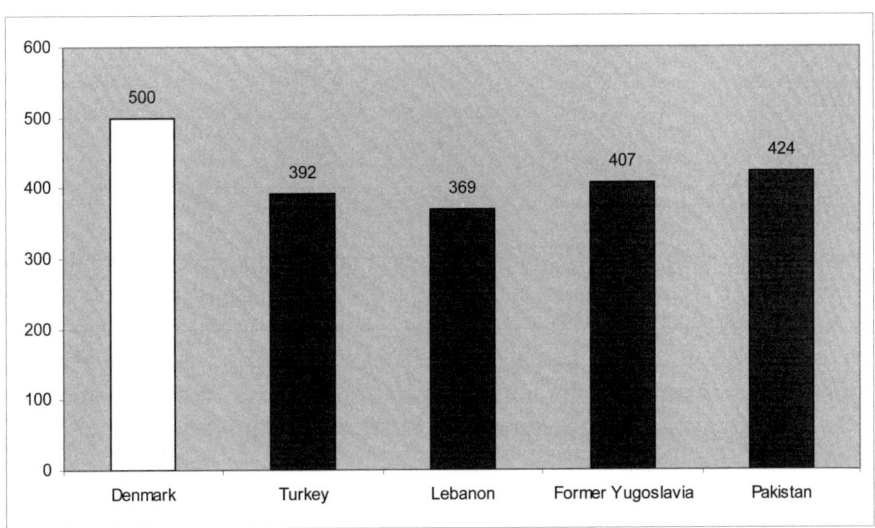

Variables of interest

The variables of interest are the coefficient estimates of the indicators of country of origin. Information on country of origin is retrieved from the administrative registers of Statistics Denmark. The distribution of the immigrant generations by country of origin is shown in Figure 3. Clearly, as mentioned above, there are some countries that have longer histories of immigration to Denmark than others. For example, only 15% of the Pakistani and 18% of the Turkish students in the dataset were born outside Denmark, while there are more equal shares of first and second generation immigrants from Lebanon and former Yugoslavia. Of the first generation immigrants from former Yugoslavia, almost 60% are Bosnians (who tend to perform better on average than the remaining students from the former Yugoslavian republics).

Figure 3. Distribution of immigrant generations by COO.

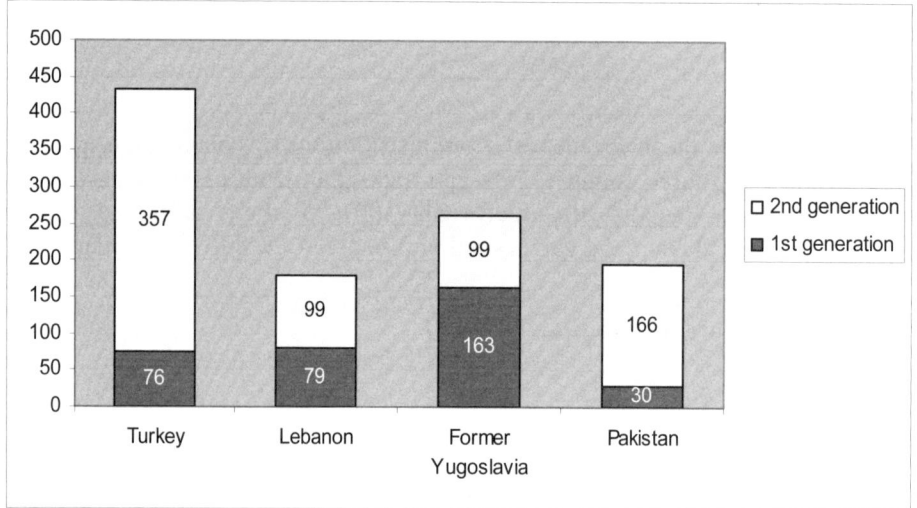

Explanatory variables

The summary statistics for the explanatory variables are displayed by country of origin in Table 1. A number of indicators show substantially different means across subsamples. Generally, the percentage of immigrant students who speak Danish at home with their parents is low[9]. Only 20% of all non-Western immigrants speak Danish at home. Students from Turkey, former Yugoslavia, and Pakistan have the highest frequency (16-19%) of using Danish as the home

---

[9] Compared to many other PISA countries, there are few immigrant families in Denmark who speak the national language at home. Among ten PISA countries (excluding Denmark), Sweden, the US and Switzerland have the largest immigrant percentages (65%, 58% and 58%) *not* speaking the national language at home, which is still far below the 80% of immigrants in Denmark who do not speak Danish at home (Schnepf 2007).

Empirical approach and data description 21

language, while students from Lebanon have the lowest propensity to do so (8%)[10]. Furthermore, for any country of origin, parental education is lower than for native Danes, but differences between countries are large. Parents from Turkey have the lowest education levels, while parents from former Yugoslavia seem to have comparatively high levels of education. Immigrants from all four source countries have a higher probability of living with both parents than Danes (67%): 74% of Lebanese students and 80% or more of students from the other three countries live with both parents.

On average, immigrant students of all source countries have more siblings than Danes, but the number varies quite a lot across countries: students from former Yugoslavia have only between 1.0-1.2 siblings (compared to 0.8 for Danes), while immigrants from Lebanon live in the largest families (with 2.6 siblings on average). The occupational status of parents from all four source countries is much lower than for Danish parents. Concerning the indicators of cultural possessions, educational resources and the number of books at home, students from all source countries score considerably lower than native Danes. However, with respect to cultural communication, Pakistani students score as highly as Danes, and so do students from former Yugoslavia for social communication.

All in all, we see great differences in student backgrounds, both compared to native Danes and across countries of origin. This highlights the importance of conditioning test score gaps on these background factors so that the estimates for countries of origin are not confounded with differences in socioeconomic backgrounds.

---

[10] A comparison of means of the groups who speak and do not speak Danish at home shows that immigrants speaking Danish at home are more likely to: (i) be second generation immigrants (69% vs. 55%), (ii) live with a single mother or father (79% vs. 72%), and (iii) have higher values on the indices of cultural communication and cultural possessions.

Table 1. Summary statistics for the explanatory variables by COO.

Variable	Danes Obs	Danes Mean	Turks Obs	Turks Mean	Lebanese Obs	Lebanese Mean	Former Yugoslavia Obs	Former Yugoslavia Mean	Pakistan Obs	Pakistan Mean
First generation (non-Western) immigrant	7511	0,00	433	0,18	178	0,44	262	0,62	196	0,15
Second generation (non-Western) immigrant	7511	0,00	433	0,82	178	0,56	262	0,38	196	0,85
Speaks Danish at home	7363	0,98	340	0,19	160	0,08	227	0,16	159	0,16
Father's years of schooling	7383	12,18	428	8,84	176	9,23	256	10,96	193	9,58
Mother's years of schooling	7483	12,22	432	7,16	178	8,48	261	10,21	195	8,47
Lives with both parents	7406	0,67	419	0,80	174	0,74	255	0,81	187	0,87
Number of siblings	7511	0,80	433	1,69	178	2,61	262	1,16	196	2,10
Highest Occupational Level of Parents (HISEI)	4575	51,25	94	34,39	35	43,49	95	35,99	79	37,53
Cultural communication	6046	0,18	340	0,01	125	0,11	180	0,03	92	0,18
Social communication	6072	0,25	345	0,07	130	0,11	183	0,27	92	0,08
Cultural possessions	6082	-0,08	345	-0,64	129	-0,64	180	-0,73	91	-0,78
Home educational resources	6115	-0,65	351	-1,32	133	-1,40	183	-1,48	93	-1,31
More than 250 books in home	6971	0,33	358	0,09	129	0,05	223	0,03	167	0,08
Cultural communication: "In general, how often do your parents: (1-5; never or hardly ever - several times a week)"										
Discuss political or social issues with you?	1266	3,13	59	2,39	37	3,35	69	2,88	90	2,77
Discuss books, films or television programmes with you?	1266	3,62	59	2,86	37	3,30	69	3,04	90	3,10
Listen to classical music with you?	1266	1,53	59	1,80	37	2,27	69	1,77	90	1,87
Social communication "In general, how often do your parents: (1-5; never or hardly ever - several times a week)"										
Discuss how well you are doing at school?	1266	4,23	59	3,98	37	4,41	69	4,32	90	4,07
Eat "the main meal" with you around a table?	1266	4,77	59	4,69	37	4,70	69	4,80	90	4,62
Spend time just talking to you?	1266	4,63	59	4,54	37	4,54	69	4,41	90	4,41

Table 1 continued.

Variable	Danes Obs	Danes Mean	Turks Obs	Turks Mean	Lebanese Obs	Lebanese Mean	Former Yugoslavia Obs	Former Yugoslavia Mean	Pakistan Obs	Pakistan Mean
Cultural possessions: "In your home, do you have: (1=yes)"										
Classical literature	1241	1,45	63	1,83	37	1,73	70	1,83	88	1,77
Books of poetry	1241	1,47	63	1,70	37	1,62	70	1,70	88	1,80
Works of art	1241	1,25	63	1,67	37	1,41	70	1,56	88	1,60
Home educational resources: "In your home, do you have:"										
A dictionary (1=yes)	1241	1,02	63	1,11	37	1,05	70	1,04	88	1,03
A quiet place to study (1=yes)	1241	1,17	63	1,29	37	1,11	70	1,20	88	1,09
A desk for study (1=yes)	1241	1,07	63	1,14	37	1,08	70	1,09	88	1,10
Text books (1=yes)	1241	1,44	63	1,75	37	1,54	70	1,77	88	1,61
How many calculators do you have in your home? (1-4; none - three or more)	1308	3,63	69	3,71	40	3,73	74	3,61	95	3,82
Years since arrival	2660	0,27	314	1,47	122	5,28	151	5,95	87	1,17
Father self-employed	2282	0,06	298	0,15	120	0,05	130	0,04	81	0,16
Father high job position	2282	0,23	298	0,01	120	0,04	130	0,02	81	0,01
Father medium/low job position	2282	0,60	298	0,45	120	0,18	130	0,58	81	0,38
Father not working	2282	0,11	298	0,39	120	0,73	130	0,36	81	0,44
Mother self-employed	2603	0,03	309	0,03	115	0,03	146	0,01	85	0,06
Mother high job position	2603	0,15	309	0,01	115	0,01	146	0,01	85	0,00
Mother medium/low job position	2603	0,68	309	0,43	115	0,10	146	0,55	85	0,20
Mother not working	2603	0,15	309	0,53	115	0,87	146	0,44	85	0,74
Mother's years of work experience in Denmark	2558	16,56	304	3,82	115	0,47	143	3,77	82	2,22
Father's years of work experience in Denmark	2272	20,34	296	8,87	120	1,35	130	7,06	80	9,22
Household income	1761	552,44	272	321,60	113	229,05	134	351,64	58	319,00

5. Estimation results

In this section, we present results from multivariate regression analyses. We first discuss results of regressions on the pooled sample of immigrant and native students, where we estimate the test score gaps corrected for differences in socioeconomic characteristics. Next, we estimate quantile regressions, which allow the coefficients to vary over the conditional test score distribution. Next, we present subsample results to allow the estimated gap to vary for different immigrant groups along various lines, e.g. by immigrant generation, gender or parental education. Finally, we consider the influence of such immigrant-specific variables as parents' years since arrival, language spoken at home and immigrant-only generation in the immigrant sample. In section 6, we propose additional explanations of the remaining test score gap.

5.1. Full sample results

Figure 2 showed that the test scores for native Danes exceed those for immigrants from all countries of origin considered in this study. If this gap narrows when we control for observable student and family characteristics, the test score gap is at least in part a result of the different socioeconomic composition of the subsamples. Ordinary Least Square estimations of equation (1) are used to test this hypothesis. For expository purposes, Figure 4 only displays estimates of the coefficients of interest, i.e. the country of origin indicators; full results are given in Table A2. To make comparisons easier, Figure 4 also presents country-coefficients from a model including only country indicators as regressors: the "raw", or uncorrected, gaps. These results mirror the gaps shown in Figure 2. The second set of results uses a set of demographic variables as the explanatory variables (student's gender; family structure, number of siblings, cultural and social communication in the family, cultural possessions and home educational resources, the number of books, household income; parents' education, occupation) along with the country of origin variables.

As we saw above, the socioeconomic characteristics of immigrants appear on average less conducive to academic achievement than those of Danes, and as expected, the corrected gaps are much smaller than the uncorrected gaps. Differences in characteristics explain about 40-50% of the difference in test scores between students with origins in Turkey, Lebanon, and former Yugoslavia and native Danish youngsters, and 65% of the difference between students from Pakistan and native Danes. Nevertheless, for all countries gaps remain both statistically significant and sizeable. For students from Lebanon, the gap is 0.80 SD, for students from Turkey and former Yugoslavia the gaps is 0.55 SD, and for Pakistan the gap is about 0.25 SD.

Figure 4. Estimates of the coefficients of interest by COO.

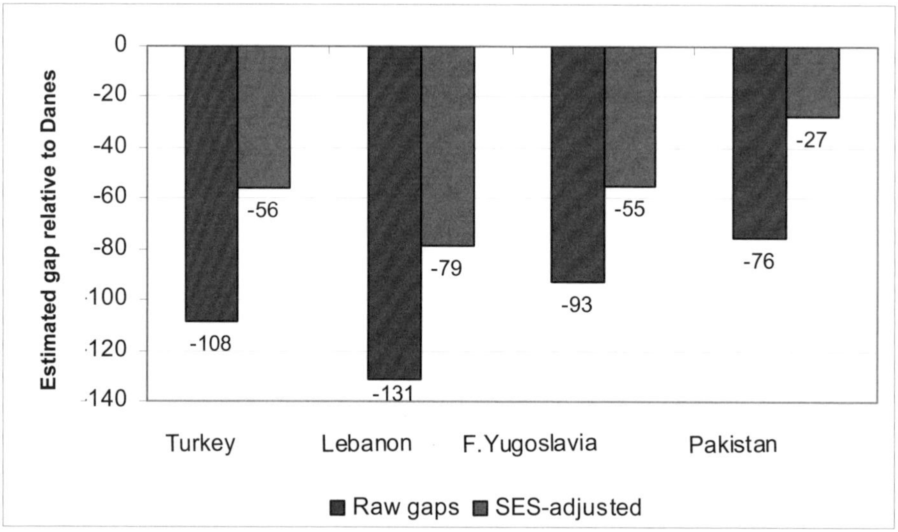

Bar chart: Estimated gap relative to Danes

- Turkey: Raw gap −108, SES-adjusted −56
- Lebanon: Raw gap −131, SES-adjusted −79
- F. Yugoslavia: Raw gap −93, SES-adjusted −55
- Pakistan: Raw gap −76, SES-adjusted −27

Legend: Raw gaps, SES-adjusted

As a robustness check, we re-estimated this regression without controls that are arguably not truly exogenous to the academic achievement of the students (i.e. cultural and social communication in the family, cultural possessions and home educational resources, the number of books). The estimated gaps were a little larger compared to the estimation including the full set of controls (see Table A2 for results). However, the additional gap explained by these additional controls is small, ranging from 3% for Turkey to 9% for former Yugoslavia. Another concern could be that there are differential cohort effects due to the fact that two of the three PISA datasets used in the pooled sample are from 2004 and 2005, while the third is from 2000. While we would not expect any substantial differences for the two consecutive years (2004, 2005), there could be differential cohort effects with the PISA dataset from 2000. To test whether the use of the 2000 data affects the results, we have re-estimated the regression above without the observations from the 2000 dataset. This reduces the immigrant sample by only 10%, because the immigrant percentage in this dataset is small (5%). Thus, we still retrieve precise estimates for the source country indicators in this reduced dataset. The results from this regression are very similar to the results from the full dataset and, as gauged by the size of the standard errors, the estimates of the source country indicators are not significantly different (see Table A2).

All in all, the results indicate that a major portion of the test score gaps can be attributed to the less favourable socioeconomic background factors of immigrant students. Nevertheless, we may still conclude that conditional on the socioeconomic status of their family, the educational achievement of all immigrant groups is poorer than that of native Danish youngsters[11].

Quantile regressions. The simple OLS model above estimates coefficients at the mean of the conditional test score distribution. However, there is no reason to believe a priori that gaps are constant over the (conditional) test score distribution. Our strategy for the estimation of heterogeneous gaps is based on the quantile regression model (equation (2)). Figure 5 shows the estimates of the country of origin coefficients from 17 quantile regressions in the range of 0.10-0.90, with increments of 0.05. The full set of covariates is included in the regressions, but only the estimates of the four country of origin indicators are shown.

Figure 5. Estimates of the COO coefficients from 17 quantile regressions.

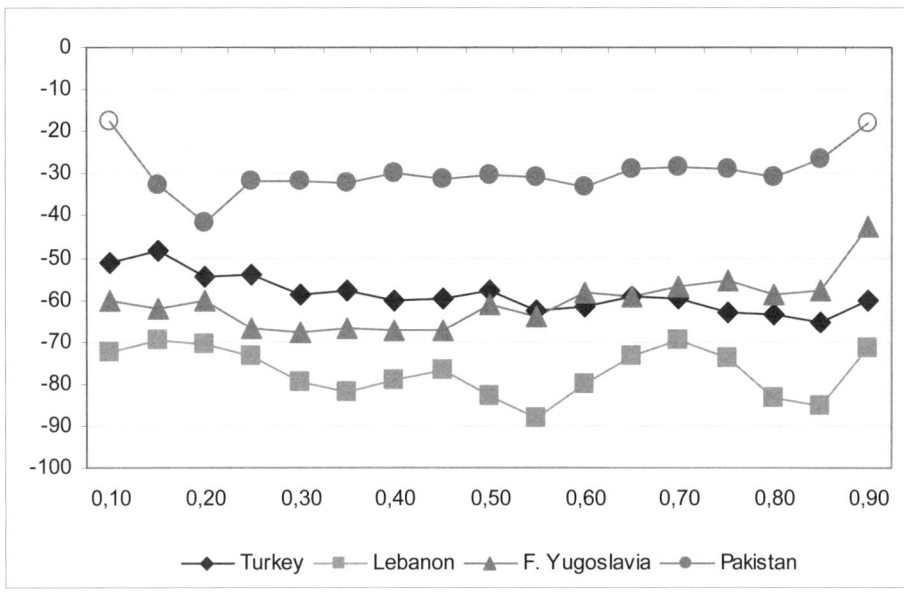

The general impression is that the quantile regressions results do not differ markedly from OLS results, since the estimates are generally similar over the

---

[11] A potential disadvantage of an analysis based on linear regressions is that observations in the different country of origin groups may not fall within a region of common support (McEwan 2008). That is to say, immigrant children may be observationally quite dissimilar from native Danish children, and the linear specification implicitly relies on projections of outcomes outside the observed range for such students. To assess the sensitivity of the results, we estimated a probit, regressing the immigrant dummy variable on the full set of family characteristics listed in Table A2. We then calculated propensity scores for each student. The region of common support includes 93% of immigrant students and 90% of Danish students. We then dropped observations that lay outside the region of common support and re-estimated the regressions from Figure 4. The estimates of the gaps were not substantively different from the full sample estimates.

conditional test score distribution[12]. Tests of whether the source country coefficients are significantly different at the lower and upper ends of the conditional test score distribution (the 0.15 and 0.85 quantiles) showed that none of the differences are significant at conventional levels[13].

5.2. Subsample results

Section 5.1 relaxed the assumption of homogenous effects across the conditional test score distribution. Another concern is that restricting the coefficient estimates to being identical across the entire sample may yield misleading results. Regressions on subsamples provide one means of addressing this concern. The results from subsample regressions displayed in Figure 6 explore the sensitivity of the estimated country of origin gaps across a variety of subsamples of the data. As before, we show only the country of origin coefficient estimates. Full sample results are available from the author upon request.

Immigrant generations. The upper left panel shows estimated test score gaps by immigrant generation. The results stem from two separate regressions. The first regression includes natives and first generation immigrants, the second includes natives and second generation immigrants. The coefficient estimates shown in Figure 6 are the source country coefficients from these regressions. Examining the performance of first and second generation immigrants from the same source country, we see that, *conditional on socioeconomic background,* the second generation from Lebanon and Pakistan does better than the first, while for Turkey, the improvement is small at best and second generation students from former Yugoslavia seem to do worse than their first generation counterparts. The relatively higher level of achievement of first generation immigrants from former Yugoslavia might be due to a composition effect, since a large share of first generation immigrants are war refugees from Bosnia, while second generation immigrants from former Yugoslavia are descendants of economic migrants[14]. Nevertheless, while the gaps are generally reduced in the second generation, they remain sizeable and significant for most source countries.

---

[12] An important assumption for quantile regression analysis is rank preservation, which means that a Danish student who has a high/low rank in test score distribution for Danes would also rank high/low in the test score distribution for immigrants "if she had an immigrant background". If this assumption, which cannot be tested, is not met, results may be biased.

[13] The Stata package in which the regressions are run does not readily accommodate cluster correction of standard errors in quantile regression analysis. Uncorrected standard errors tend to be too small. However, since the statistic of interest (i.e. the difference between source country estimates at the lower and upper ends of the distribution) is non-significant even with uncorrected errors, correcting the standard errors would render the statistic even less significant, which would leave unchanged the conclusion that the COO gaps are stable over the test score distribution.

[14] We cannot identify the ethnic composition of second generation migrants, since they all are coded as coming from Yugoslavia before the country was split up.

Language at home. In the PISA questionnaire, students stated whether they mostly speak Danish or language other than Danish in the family. Using Danish at home might help improve language skills, a factor which is likely to translate into higher reading literacy scores. Over and above the effect on language proficiency, speaking Danish at home might also be an indicator of a higher level of integration into the Danish society. The results in the second panel of Figure 6 show that, as expected, for many source countries, students who mainly speak Danish at home do better compared to those who speak their heritage language at home. In fact, the test score gap is actually reduced to zero for Danish-speaking families from former Yugoslavia and Pakistan. On the other hand, for students from Lebanon and particularly from Turkey test scores do not greatly differ in families who do or do not speak Danish. However, these results cannot readily be given a clear causal interpretation, since we cannot distinguish causal effects from selection effects of speaking Danish at home. In spite of the encouraging results for Danish-speaking families from former Yugoslavia and Pakistan, the size of these groups is small, since only 16% of immigrant families from these countries use Danish as their main family language.

By gender. In some of the source countries, girls' education is not given the same priority as that of boys, and getting girls to school is a challenge because of gender discrimination and cultural traditions. Girls are expected to work inside the home and look after their younger brothers and sisters, and they are sometimes forced into early marriage. These differences become evident in the literacy rates: for example, recent figures for Pakistan show that 62% of males but only 35% of females can read and write (Table 3, section 6.3). Further, for first generation immigrants, the experience of malnutrition prior to migration may have hindered them from reaping the full benefits from their home country schooling, and malnutrition might also have persistent impacts on their intellectual ability. Malnutrition is more severe among girls than among boys in many countries (Banerjee & Bandyopadhyay, 2005; Schoenbaum et al., 1995; Zere & McIntyre, 2003). In addition, school quality in the source countries might not be as high as in developed countries, due to poorer financial and human resources. Moreover, due to cultural bias and single-sex schooling, school quality might be lower for girls than for boys. Thus, immigrant girls in Denmark may need special attention. However, we would expect the impact from these disadvantages to be smaller for second generation students, even though cultural gender bias might persist through intergenerational transmission even for students born in Denmark.

To consider these possible gender differences, we present evidence on source country gaps for boys and girls from separate regressions. The results are shown in the third panel of Figure 6. The analysis shows that the test score gap relative to native Danes is larger for girls than for boys from Turkey and to a lesser extent from Lebanon, while there are only small gender differences for

Figure 6. Subsample regressions.

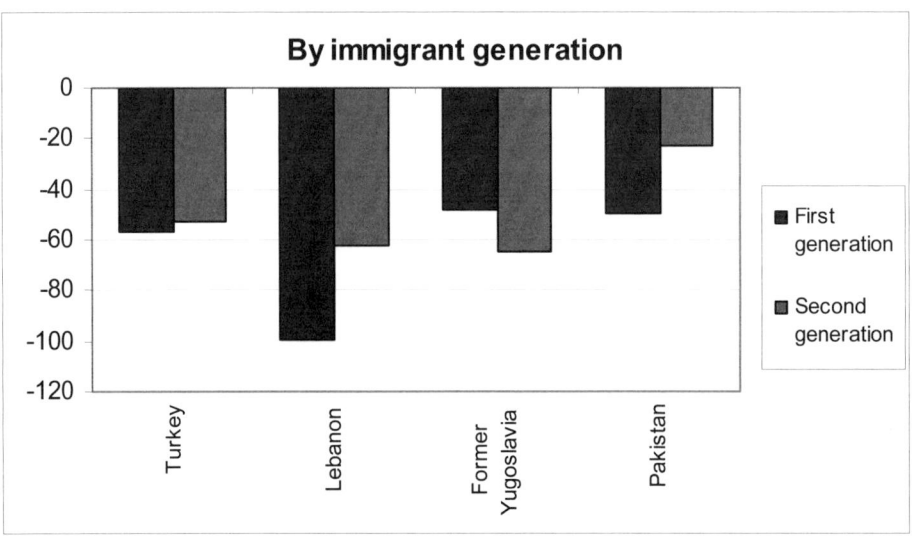

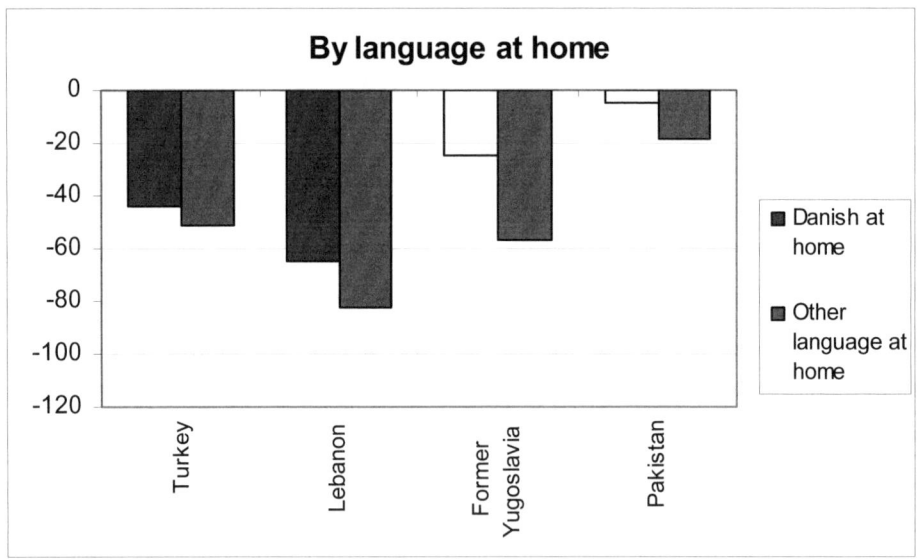

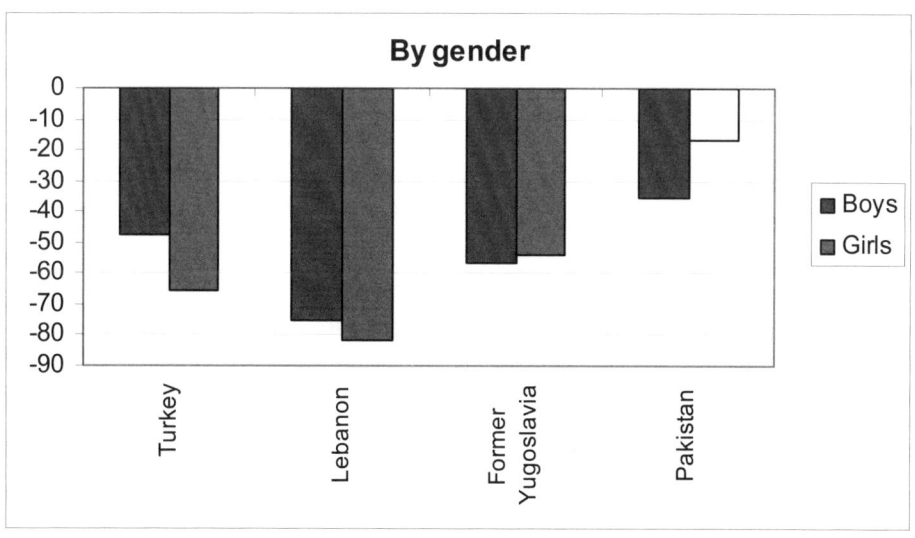

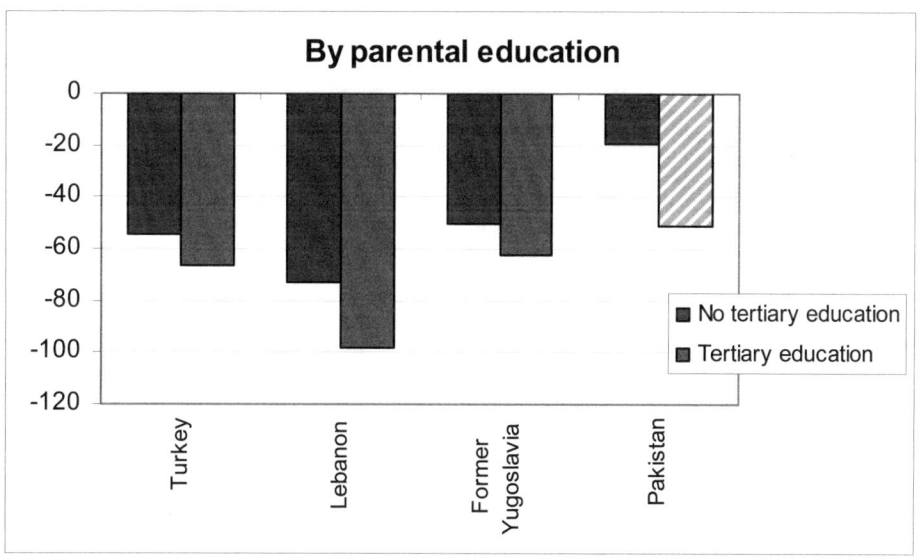

Note: Solid bars indicate significance at the 5% level. Hatched bars indicate significance at the 10% level.

students from former Yugoslavia. Interestingly, for Pakistan the gender gap is reversed: boys under-perform compared to otherwise similar Danish boys, while there is no significant gap for girls. We have tried to further investigate whether gender gaps close in the second generation, but the results turn out to be weak, probably due to small sample sizes, and are not reported. Thus, gender differences seem to exist for students from Turkey and to a lesser extent for students from Lebanon (in favour of boys) and Pakistan (in favour of girls), so that girls or boys from these countries might need special attention.

By parental education. To investigate whether the gap to Danes differs across parental education levels, we ran regressions separately for students with parents with low and high levels of education (last panel of Fig. 6)[15]. Interestingly, the general picture is that the gap relative to natives is larger for students from more well-educated families, i.e. those with at least some tertiary education. However, the gap relative to native Danes is only marginally significant for children from highly educated families from Pakistan.

Immigrant subsample. As mentioned above, we do not include immigrant-specific variables in the full sample regressions, because they are either constant or not even defined for native Danes. However, since the influence of these variables may be determinants of immigrants' test scores, they are of interest in their own right. We therefore present results from the immigrant subsample in Table 2. Two specifications are estimated: one with country of origin indicators, the other without. Both specifications include all controls from the main model above, plus an indicator of the language used at home (Danish/other), the number of years since arrival in Denmark for the student's father and mother (and their squared terms), and whether the student was born in Denmark (second generation) or not (first generation). Years since migration for the students themselves is not included, since this variable is not defined for the second generation.

Results for the immigrant subsample both with and without source country dummies are presented in Table 2. Generally, the results do not differ whether source country dummies are included or not. However, some estimates are significant predictors only in regressions which exclude source country dummies. This suggests, for example, that the negative effect of the number of children is not so much related to students in large families attaining lower scores, but to large families originating mainly from source countries with lower average performance. As the results show, among the immigrant-specific variables, only mother's years since arrival is significant (even in a regression without controls.).

---

[15] Lower level education is 'no parent tertiary education', while higher level education indicates 'at least one parent with some tertiary education'.

Table 2. Immigrant subsample results

	Coef.	Robust Std. Err	P>|t|	Coef.	Robust Std. Err	P>|t|
Female	**18,389**	4,373	0,000	**17,476**	4,474	0,000
Father: years of schooling	**1,888**	0,534	0,000	**1,968**	0,568	0,001
Mother: years of schooling	0,467	0,473	0,324	0,661	0,455	0,148
Lived with both parents	4,469	5,649	0,430	5,537	5,748	0,336
No. siblings	-2,238	1,773	0,208	**-3,766**	1,806	0,038
Occupational status (index)	0,211	0,222	0,342	0,237	0,225	0,292
Cultural communication	**7,197**	3,001	0,017	**7,727**	3,029	0,011
Social communication	3,893	3,201	0,225	2,264	3,189	0,478
Cultural posessions	3,765	2,987	0,209	2,414	3,041	0,428
Home educational resources	**6,138**	2,585	0,018	**6,501**	2,571	0,012
No. books at home	5,566	10,069	0,581	9,666	10,163	0,342
Father:						
Self-employed	*Reference*			*Reference*		
High occup. status	*74,294*	*18,101*	*0,000*	*75,720*	*18,336*	*0,000*
Middle/low occup. status	*27,217*	*13,877*	*0,051*	*27,262*	*14,084*	*0,054*
Not working	*20,612*	*11,741*	*0,080*	*19,683*	*11,867*	*0,098*
Mother:						
Self-employed						
High occup. Status	*47,492*	*26,964*	*0,079*	28,972	28,419	0,309
Middle/low occup. status	1,006	14,714	0,946	-14,128	15,713	0,369
Not working	-18,926	15,462	0,222	**-33,820**	16,795	0,045
Mother: years of labour market experience	1,307	1,081	0,228	0,890	1,131	0,432
Father: years of labour market experience	-0,007	0,733	0,993	0,117	0,740	0,874
Household income/1000	0,014	0,027	0,595	0,026	0,027	0,329
Danish is main language at home	4,800	6,609	0,468	*10,719*	6,250	0,088
Father: years since immigration	-2,831	2,944	0,337	-2,925	3,047	0,338
Square-term ----- " -------------	0,030	0,071	0,669	0,043	0,074	0,563
Mother: years since immigration	**9,021**	2,624	0,001	**7,618**	2,541	0,003
Square-term ----- " -------------	**-0,241**	0,068	0,000	**-0,200**	0,066	0,003
Second generation	1,459	6,458	0,821	6,012	6,283	0,340
Constant	355,062	50,475	0,000	356,409	50,558	0,000
COO-indicators included?	Yes			No		
Number of observations	1892			1892		
R-squared	0,196			0,161		

Note: Missing value flags and single items of composites are included in all regressions.

6. Why do immigrants with similar socio-economic background underperform compared to Danes?

In this section, we explore some additional factors that might explain some of the unexplained gap between native Danes and immigrants from different countries of origin. First, we add school fixed effects to account for the fact that students are not distributed randomly across schools and that schools differ in a variety of aspects which might affect achievement over and above students' own socioeconomic backgrounds. Next, we present an exploratory analysis of differences in attitudes and expectations towards education, family and work life between native Danes and immigrants from different countries of origin in order to examine whether these differences are related to test score gaps. Last, we discuss some additional possible explanations such as ethnic capital in Denmark and the home country and aspects of family formation patterns (consanguineous marriages).

6.1. Do immigrants attend different (and worse) schools?

In order to test whether schools matter for the native-immigrant test score gaps, in this section we present results of regressions taking account of school fixed effects. This allows us to remove any observable as well as unobservable effects that are fixed within schools. In particular, the student composition differs greatly in schools attended by native Danes and immigrant students, which might affect reading scores if peer effects matter. For example, in our dataset only 5% of native Danish students attend schools with a majority of immigrant students, while more than 50% of students from Lebanon and Pakistan, and about 40% of students from Turkey and former Yugoslavia do so. In addition, while native Danish students attend schools with peers whose parents on average have 13 years of education, students from the four countries of origin attend schools with peers whose parents on average have only about 11.6 to 12.0 years of schooling. These results suggest that there are systematic differences between Danish and immigrant students' schools. The following school fixed effects estimations control for these differences.

The coefficient estimates for the country of origin indicators from a regression including the full set of socioeconomic characteristics and school fixed effects are illustrated in Figure 7, along with those results from the main model in section 5.1. which include only socioeconomic characteristics. The pattern shows that, as one would expect, including school fixed effects reduces the gap estimates for all countries. This suggests that schools mostly attended by immigrants are associated with lower academic achievement than schools attended mainly by native Danes. However, school fixed effects explain only a small additional part of the remaining gap once socioeconomic characteristics are included. The coefficients of the country of origin indicators remain significant and decrease only little. Thus, differences between schools do not explain much of the remaining gap.

Figure 7. School fixed-effects regression.

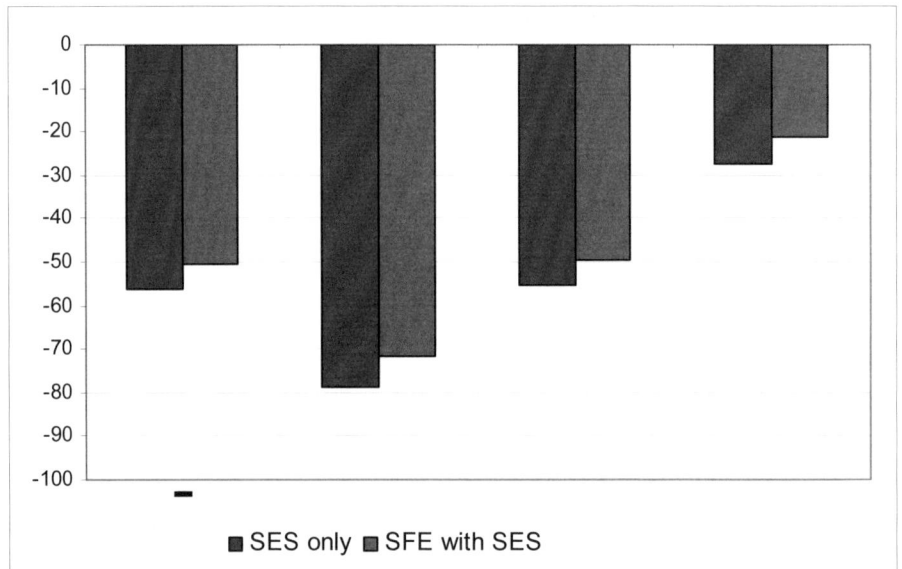

6.2. Difference in attitudes and expectations

In this section, we investigate differences in attitudes and expectations towards family formation and compatibility between family life and employment. As part of the PISA Ethnic assessment, the 9th graders were asked a range of questions like: do you think that (i) your future spouse has the same religion as you, (ii) your future spouse is born in Denmark/Europe/your country of origin, (iii) your parents have introduced you to your future partner/had the decisive word in your choice of partner, (iv) you will have many children, (v) it is important to complete an education before having children, (vi) it is important that your future spouse works mostly at home, and (vii) the mother will stay at home with your children while they are young (and after that).

All these factors can be thought of as serving as proxies for a more or less conservative life style which is orientated towards the culture of the source country, where women need not invest in a lot of education because they expect to marry at a young age and stay at home to raise their children and do the housework. While a conservative orientation might explain lower educational achievement for girls, it is not obvious why these factors should be correlated with lower achievement for boys, too. However, we suggest two channels through which these factors might affect boys as well. First, these factors may be broad indicators of a cultural (and educational) distance of the home country culture to the Western culture[16], where education and labour market success are

---

[16] Or among the specific, selected group of individuals from these countries who chose to emigrate to Denmark.

key elements in society. Second, boys may also be affected directly because, as Böcker (1994) suggests, if arranged marriages between youngsters who have grown up in Denmark and spouses from the home country are common – which recent research suggests is the case (Nielsen et al., 2007) – being a permanent resident of Denmark and thus being able to provide access to life in a Western country might be enough to be an attractive partner in the marriage market. Moreover, if a man imports a spouse, he may sacrifice his own education to be able to support the imported spouse.

Information on attitudes and expectations is available only for the PISA Ethnic assessment. Obviously, this also reduces the sample size, which is one reason why this analysis can be only exploratory of nature, and not a rigorous assessment. The other important reason is the possible endogeneity between the attitudes and expectations variables and students' test scores. Therefore, our results cannot readily be given a causal explanation, since attitudes and expectations towards family formation and working life at the end of compulsory schooling are hardly exogenous to contemporaneous educational achievement. Although the estimated relationship will not imply strict causality, the results will illuminate the relationships between attitudes and expectations and the native-immigrant test score gap.

We start this exploratory analysis by presenting the data. First, we show raw frequencies by country of origin separately for boys and girls. In the questionnaire, the responses fall into five categories: entirely agree; partly agree; agree and disagree; partly disagree, entirely disagree. For ease of comparison, we have pooled the answers *entirely agree/partly agree* into one category and the remaining three answers into another category. As always with subjective assessments, answers might be coloured by the ethnic (or social) context in which a student has been raised. For example, some questions may be differently understood by native Danes and by immigrants, so differences in frequencies cannot be easily interpreted. For example, students are asked the question *do you expect to have many children?* For native Danes, this probably means having more than two children, while for Lebanese, for example, who on average have much larger families, "many" might signify a much higher number.

Other questions are also somewhat difficult/awkward, since they were implicitly meant to be directed at certain groups, but have been posed to all students. For example, asking (immigrant) girls whether they expect their future spouse to stay at home while their children are young is clearly not the information sought after – the information wanted is answers to the same question when posed to boys. Despite these problems, in the following we present results for all questions posed to both boys and girls.

Figures 8 and 9 show frequencies by gender for the two categories. Some of the interesting results from the frequency tables are that the majority of students from all source countries agree (entirely or partly) that their future spouse/partner has the same religious background as themselves (60-90%). The

Figure 8. Students' expectations to their future spouse and to the form of marriage.

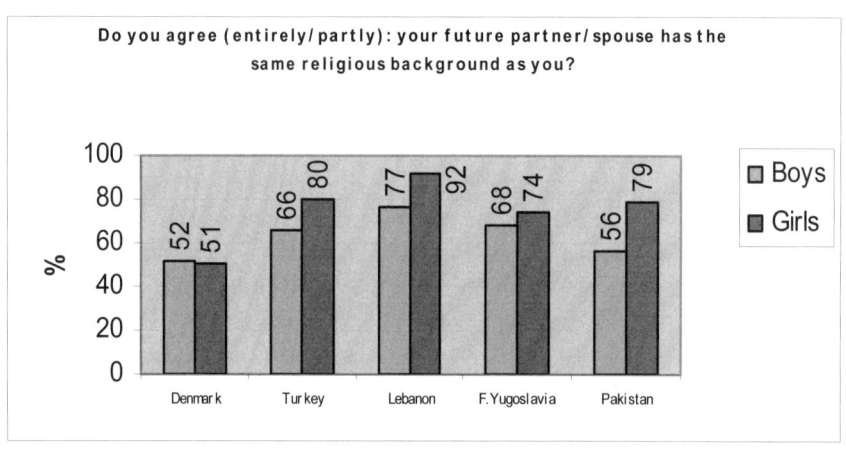

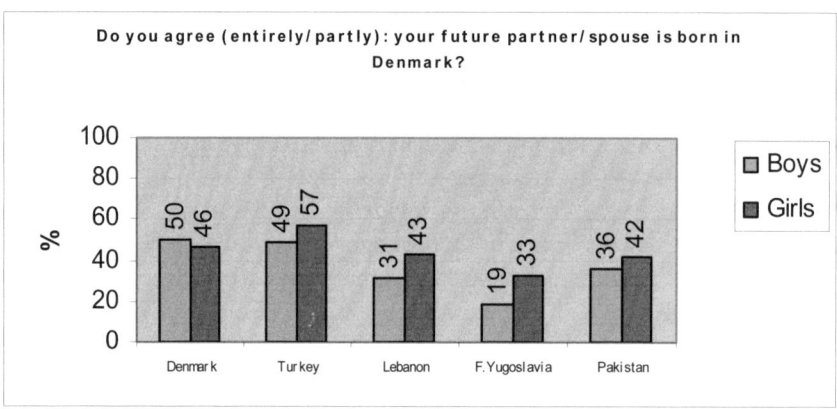

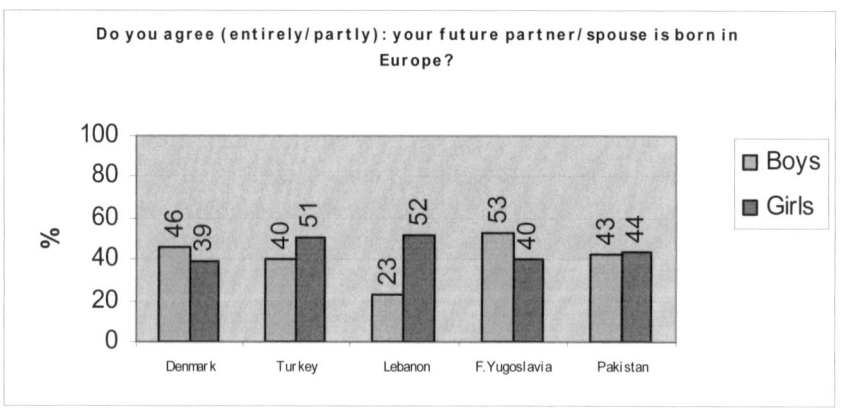

Figure 8 continued.

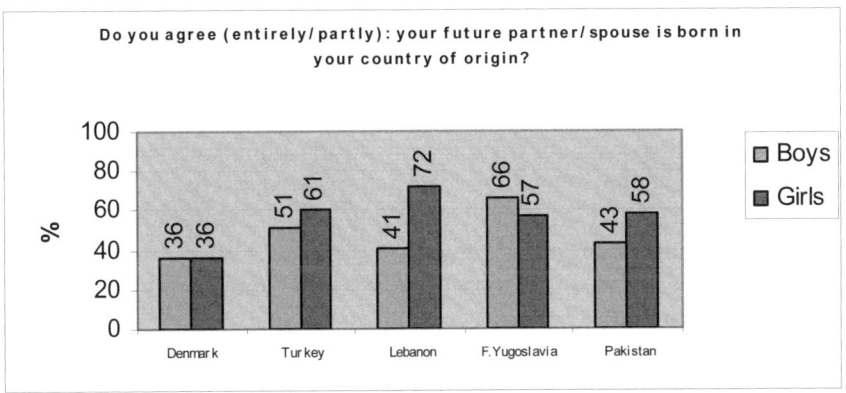

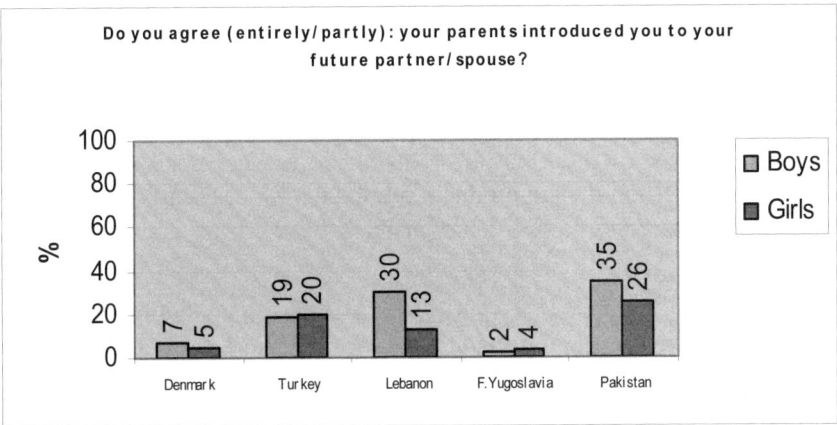

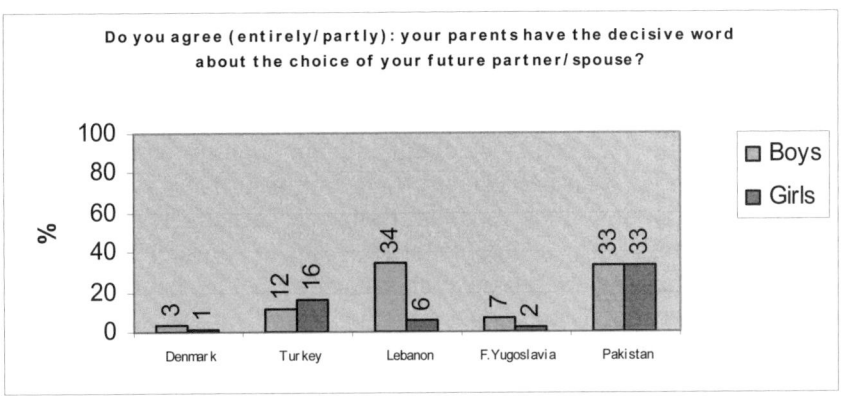

share for girls is somewhat higher than for boys. Interestingly, 50% of native Danes also expect to marry a partner of the same religion as themselves. On the other hand, given that almost all Danes share the same religion, this number is hardly surprising, since the supply of potential spouses of Lutheran affiliation is clearly the largest in Denmark.

When students are asked whether they agree with the statement that their future spouse is born in their country of origin, the pattern of answers is similar to that for the question of religious background, but the share is generally smaller. Interestingly, the results suggest that only 40% of native Danes expect to marry a partner born in Denmark. Surprisingly, only a few immigrants expect their parents to introduce them to their partner or to have the decisive word about the choice of their partner. In contrast to these results, existing studies using statistics from the Danish administrative registers show that a large majority of young immigrants from Turkey and Pakistan marry "imported" spouses, i.e. partners from their country of origin who emigrate to Denmark to marry an immigrant with a Danish residence permit. Furthermore, it is common knowledge that a large number of these marriages are arranged marriages. However, it may be that these practices are so embedded in the immigrant culture that they are not perceived as parent-arranged marriages by the young immigrants themselves, or they may be reluctant to answer positively to these questions given the current debate on this issue in Denmark. Finally, maybe they truly expect that these patterns will have changed by the time they get married themselves.

When students are asked whether they want to have many children, Danish students seem to be the most enthusiastic (!) – Figure 9, upper panel. About 60% of native Danes indicate that they want to have many children. The numbers for the other countries of origin vary by country and gender, but generally range between 30 and 50%. Yet, as mentioned above, we cannot conclude from this that Danes actually are going to have more children than immigrants, since the number of children perceived as "many" may vary significantly across countries and cultures. It is interesting to note though that having large families does not generally seem to be a top priority among immigrant youth.

Completing an education before having children is important for at least 70% of students from all source countries (Figure 9, second panel). Females from all countries are similarly ambitious on their husbands' behalf (Figure 9, third panel), while boys from some source countries seem to consider it somewhat less important that their wives complete an education before having children. While the distance to native Danes is not large when students are asked whether they agree that the mother should stay at home while the children are young[17] (Figure 9, fifth panel), substantially larger shares of boys from Turkey, Lebanon and former Yugoslavia believe that their future spouse will stay at home with the

---

[17] Still, the definition of young children might be perceived very differently by different groups, with native Danes maybe returning to work earlier after childbirth.

children. Differences are also greater regarding staying permanently at home: around 40% of males from Turkey and Lebanon agree that the mother should stay at home both while the children are young and afterwards. Perhaps encouragingly, the corresponding numbers for females are much lower (Fig. 9, last panel). Clearly, girls are much more keen on the idea of mothers working for pay than are their potential future husbands.

To conclude, there are some interesting differences across countries of origin in attitudes and expectations. In the next step, we investigate whether these differences can explain some of the test score gaps between natives and immigrants that remain after socioeconomic differences and school fixed effects are taken into account. As mentioned above, the answers to a few of the questions posed may be plagued by cultural bias, e.g. asking students whether they want to have many children[18], or whether the mother should stay at home while the children are young. The *true* difference between native Danes and immigrants in the number of children wanted, or the actual time (in months or years) the mother stays at home with their young children, is probably larger than measured by the answers to these questions. If the wish for many children, or the time spent at home to raise children, is related to lower test scores, the direction of the bias will tend to underestimate the reduction in the gap relative to native Danes in an estimation of the test score gaps that include this variable. According to these reflections, we are more likely to *under*estimate the importance of the attitudes and expectations variables than to overestimate it.

Estimation Results

Results from estimating equation (5) including the attitudes and expectation indicators are illustrated in Figure 10[19]. As before, the bars represent the estimates of the country of origin indicators. The baseline results (with SES controls only) and results including SES and school fixed effects are included in Figure 10, too, for ease of comparison. For all countries except for former Yugoslavia, the inclusion of the attitudes and expectations variables in the regression explains an additional part of the remaining gap relative to native Danes.

---

[18] The difference between native Danes and immigrants in the number of children wanted is probably larger than is measured by the answers.
[19] For the estimations, the five categories for the answers are preserved. For simplicity, we enter the equations as a linear variable, rather than as sets of dummy variables, which would be a more flexible specification.

Figure 9. Students' expectations regarding their future family and working life.

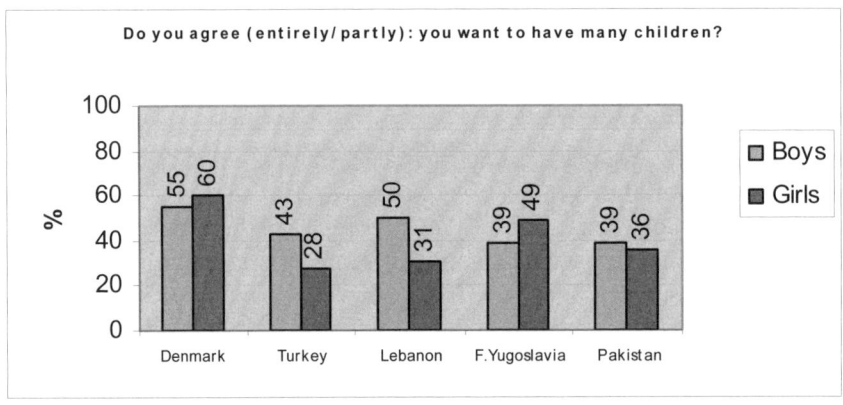

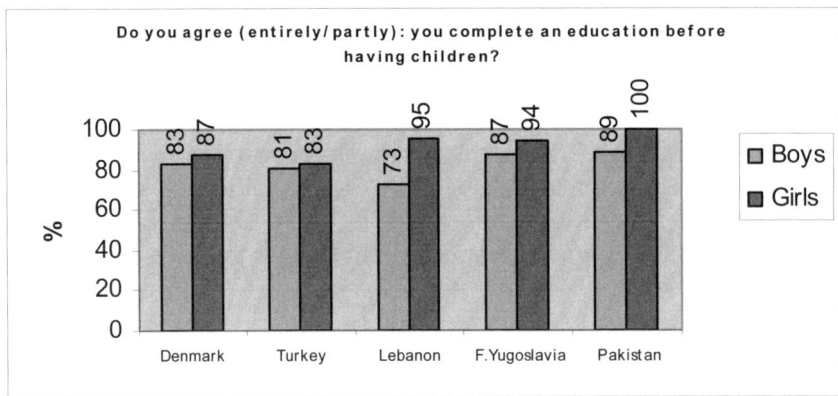

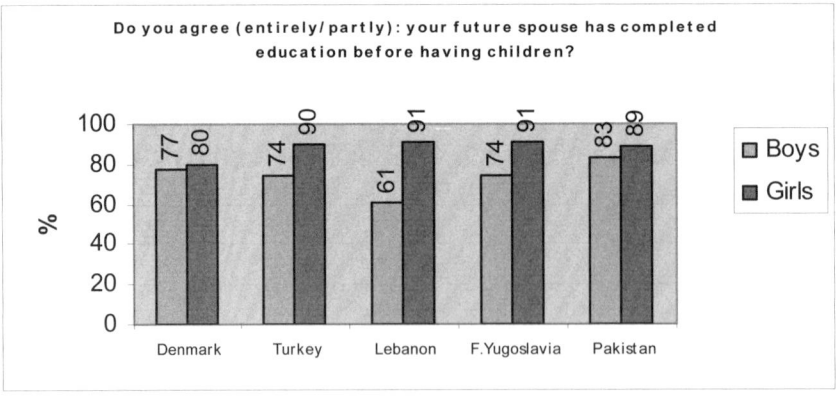

Figure 9 continued.

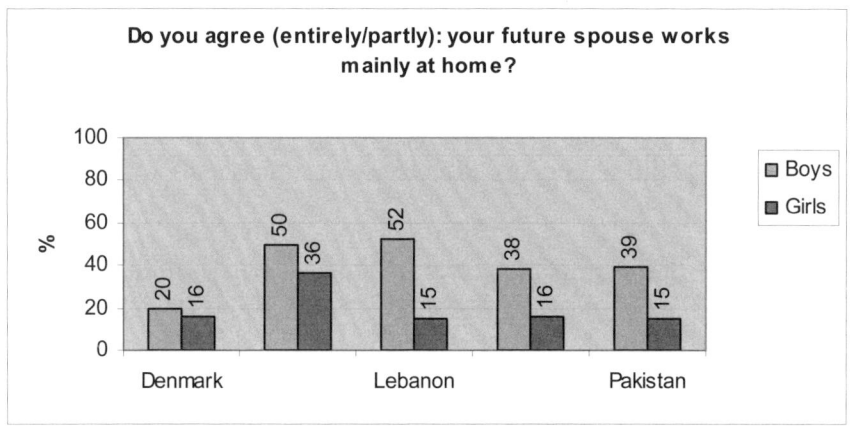

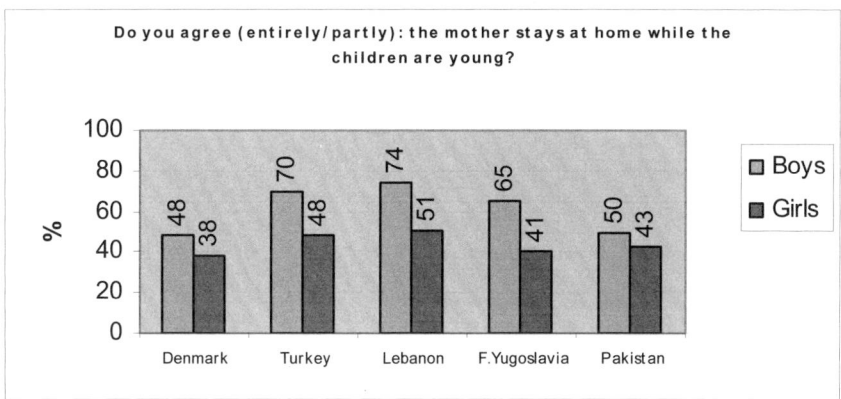

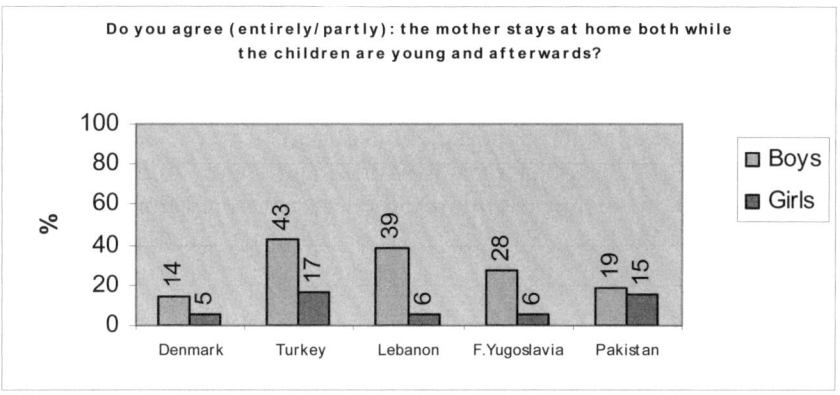

The partial conclusion from this analysis is that cultural differences concerning family formation, children and working life explain part of the remaining gap, so: cultural differences matter. But as mentioned above, we cannot be sure that these results are not at least partly driven by mere correlation[20]. Also, for all countries but Pakistan, the gaps stay large and significant, meaning that an important part of the gap cannot be explained by differences in socioeconomic background, school differences or differences in (measured) attitudes and expectations.

Figure 10. Estimation-results including attitudes & expectations variables.

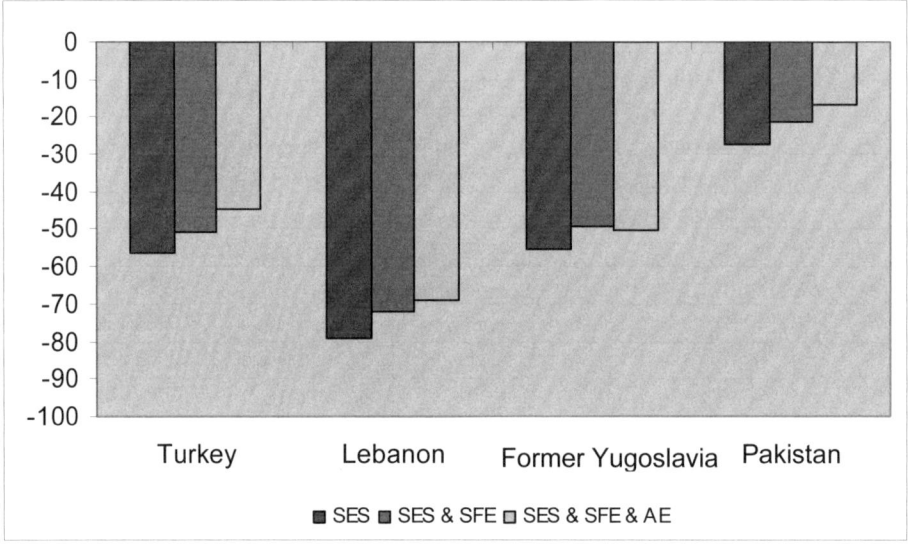

When we run the analysis above separately for boys and girls, we can investigate whether including the attitudes and expectations variables has a different impact by gender. Results from such subsample regressions are shown in Figure 11. In most cases, adding attitudes and expectations reduces the gap relative to native Danes. The decrease of the gap is largest for Turkish girls and for Pakistani boys for whom the gap is now no longer significantly different from zero.

---

[20] It would probably be preferable to include country means of these variables, but unfortunately, we cannot include other variables that vary at the country level only together with our country of origin dummies.

Figure 11. Estimation-results including attitudes & expectations variables by gender.

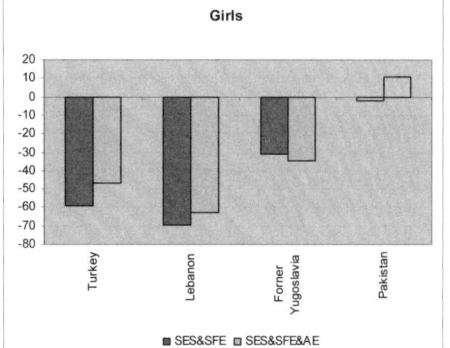

6.3. Additional possible factors behind the gap

In this section, we suggest several other factors that might be related to the test score gap. However, since this information is available only at the country level, the factors cannot be entered directly into our main regression together with the country of origin indicators, which are the main variables of interest[21]. As argued above, cultural differences regarding education between source countries and between boys and girls may be related to the remaining gaps. Therefore, in this section, we consider two sets of factors: (i) indicators of ethnic capital concerning educational standards in the source country, and (ii) indicators of ethnic capital concerning educational standards of compatriots in Denmark to account for the possibility that a selective group of the source country has migrated to Denmark, and that it is the human capital of co-ethnics in Denmark that influences students' achievement. In addition, we consider two factors related to family formation. First, marriage migration is quite frequent among some immigrant groups. This could impact on children's educational attainment, since this means having one parent who did not grow up and was not educated in Denmark and is therefore probably less proficient in Danish and has less knowledge of the Danish society in general and of the education system in particular. As also mentioned above, being a resident in Denmark might be enough to make a person attractive as a potential spouse for compatriots in the home country, while education might be considered secondary. This can be a disincentive to invest in education for young immigrants from countries where marriage migration is common.

Another consideration is that marrying a near relative is a widespread practice in some source countries. Consanguineous marriage between first cousins has been shown to be related to various health problems of the offspring, e.g. developmental delays, morbidity, genetic disorders, and even mortality (e.g.

---

[21] Obviously, we could do a second stage regression at the country level, but this seems not very promising with so few observations at the country level.

Kandamuthan, 1997). Learning disability is also often related explicitly to consanguineous marriage. Specifically, Abu-Rabia & Maroun (2005) show that the rate of reading disabilities among children of first-cousin parents was higher than that for children of unrelated parents.[22]

Ethnic capital in the source country

Blau, Kahn & Papps (2008) show that labour market participation rates of female immigrants are closely related to labour market participation rates in their home country, and that this is constant regardless of time in the US. Men's labour supply assimilation profiles are unaffected by source country female labour supply, a result that suggests that the female findings reflect notions of gender roles rather than overall work orientation. This is evidence of a persistence of home country gender roles even when immigrants have lived in the host country for many years, and this might explain some of the source country and gender gaps in their children, too.

Table 3 shows average values of the above-mentioned factors by country of origin. First, we consider measures of ethnic educational capital in the source countries. We consider the following indicators: the percentage of adults (males and females) who are literate, enrolment rates in primary, secondary and tertiary education, the percentage of adults who did not go to school, school life expectancy (years) and the gender parity index[23] (source: Edstats, Worldbank). Table 3 shows that while male literacy is high (>90%) in Denmark, Turkey and Lebanon, only about 60% of males are literate in Pakistan. Female literacy rates are somewhat lower than in Denmark in Turkey and Lebanon, while only one out of three women in Pakistan is literate. Primary school enrolment is high (>90%) in all countries (Pakistan slightly lower).

Secondary school rates are little lower in Turkey and former Yugoslavia compared to Denmark, while Pakistan has much lower secondary school rates (27%). Tertiary education enrolment rates are much lower than in Denmark in all countries, and are close to zero in Pakistan. An interesting indicator is also the gender parity index (ratio of girls to boys in primary/secondary education), suggesting that males attend primary and secondary education at much higher rates than females in Pakistan. While these numbers give information about the educational level of the current young generations, the two last rows are an indicator of the level for the adult population, i.e. the generations who are parents to the students in our study. While only 12% of adults in former Yugoslavia did not go to school at all, the number is higher for Turks (28%) and

---

[22] Even though many students with special education needs were excluded from the PISA assessment, learning disabilities may be more or less severe. Students with milder learning disabilities would therefore be likely to be included in the PISA assessment.

[23] Gender parity index = gross enrolment ratio in primary and secondary education.

substantially higher for Pakistanis (70%). For all countries, the percentage of females who did not go to school is higher than for males.

Ethnic capital among compatriots in Denmark

The second set of ethnic capital covariates describes the educational level of compatriots in Denmark. We have calculated the percentages of mothers and fathers who are unskilled (no more than lower secondary education), who have (some) tertiary education, who are (permanently) out of the labour force and those who have only weak attachment to the labour market (i.e. who are unemployed more than half the year) using administrative records of a 100% sample of three generations of students (those in 9th grade in 2002-2004), Table 3, middle part.

As suspected, there seem to be specific subgroups of the population who migrated to Denmark. While the total population in Turkey is among the best educated of all source countries (Table 3, upper part), the immigrant population from Turkey in Denmark is among the least educated: the percentage of unskilled fathers and mothers is the highest and the percentage with tertiary education is the lowest among the four countries of origin.

While the total population in Pakistan is the least educated among the four countries of origin, those who decided to emigrate to Denmark are placed comfortably in the middle: Pakistanis have a lower share of unskilled parents and about the same percentage of highly-educated parents as Turkish parents in Denmark, but lag far behind parents from former Yugoslavia. The percentage of fathers and mothers who are not in the labour force or who have only a weak attachment to the labour market (defined as those who were unemployed for more than half of the year when the child was 12 years old) varies a lot across countries. The percentages of mothers and fathers who are outside the labour force range from 26% and 12% in Turkey to 72% and 51% in Lebanon. An additional 9% to 17% have only a weak attachment to the labour market.

Table 3. Ethnic capital differences and family formation.

		Denmark	Turkey	Lebanon	Former Yugoslavia	Pakistan
Ethnic capital of compatriots in home-country						
Male literacy		99%	94%	93%	.	62%
Female literacy		99%	79%	82%	.	35%
Primary school enrolment [1]		101%	93%	107%	100%	82%
Secondary school enrolment [1]		124%	79%	89%	90%	27%
Tertiary school enrolment [1]		75%	29%	48%	42%	3%
Gender parity index		1	0,9	1	1	0,7
% of **female** population aged 25 and above who did not attend school (2000) – Barro&Lee, Worldbank		0%	36%	.	19%	84%
% of **total** population aged 25 and above who did not attend school (2000) – Barro&Lee, Worldbank		0%	28%	.	12%	70%
Ethnic capital of compatriots in Denmark						
Max. lower secondary education (%) [2]	Mother	29%	74%	67%	34%	64%
	Father	24%	69%	43%	17%	46%
Tertiary education - short, medium or long (%) [2]	Mother	16%	5%	10%	15%	7%
	Father	26%	2%	6%	11%	3%
Out of labour force (%)	Mother	7%	26%	72%	42%	46%
	Father	5%	12%	51%	32%	24%
Weak attachment to labour market (%) [3]	Mother	4%	17%	9%	9%	17%
	Father	2%	17%	11%	9%	13%
Family formation						
Marriage migration (Çelikaksoy et al)		.	~ 90%	.	.	~ 80%
Consanguineous marriages in Norway (Surén et al., 2007)		.	27%	.	.	55%
Consanguineous marriages in Great Britain (City of Bradford) Corry (2002)		.	.	.	.	50-60%
Consanguineous marriages in source countries (Bittles 2008)		.	20-29%	.	.	>50%

[1] The gross enrolment ratio is calculated by expressing the number of students enrolled in primary, secondary and tertiary levels of education, regardless of age, as a percentage of the population of official school age for the three levels. This measure can exceed 100%, if an education level enrols students who are older than the typical age for this education.

[2] For many immigrants, the level of education is missing in the register information. Percentages of missing information range from 29% for Turkish women to 6% for men from former Yugoslavia. Only observations with no missing information on education enter the calculation of parents' level of education presented here.

[3] Employees with more than 50% unemployment per year.

Note: The statistics for labour market attachment are not directly comparable with those used in Table 1, since they originate from different statistical sources.

Family formation

Marrying a near relative is common practice in a number of non-Western countries. Yet this practice has been linked to higher risks of prenatal losses, early mortality, morbidity and genetic disorders in the children from such unions. Such consequences can be more or less severe. While students with severe disorders are not included in the PISA assessment (and thus cannot be a source of the observed test score gaps), students with milder learning disorders or morbidity may well be included in our estimation sample.

If there is a higher prevalence of such students among immigrants than among native Danes due to "more risky" marriage behaviour, these differences may be able to explain an additional part of the test score gaps. However, statistics related to this issue are rare, and are non-existent for Denmark. One piece of evidence comes from a recent Norwegian study (Surén et al. 2007), which suggests that 55% of Pakistanis living in Norway are married to a relative, as are 27% of Turks. Another, more local study of Pakistanis in the city of Bradford, Great Britain, estimates that between 50 and 60% are married to a near relative (Corry 2002). While statistics on consanguineous marriages among immigrant populations in Western countries are rare, estimates of the frequencies among the total resident populations in various countries from which Europe has drawn immigrants exist.

These estimates confirm a high incidence of consanguineous marriages for some source countries: more than 50% of Pakistanis (in Pakistan) marry a close relative, as do 20-29% of Turks (Table 3). Data on family formation for Denmark is still rare. Yet, the (few) existing numbers suggest that, for example, the incidence of marriage migration is frequent in some subgroups, particularly for Turkey and Pakistan, and these marriages are often with a near relative. Celikaksoy et al. (2007) show than around 80% of the young immigrant women and more than 50% of young immigrant men marry a marriage migrant in their first marriage. Although we cannot assess the importance for reading score gaps of these additional factors, they may matter, and obviously they are interesting candidates to be considered in future research.

7. Conclusion

As a new feature in PISA research, we are able to analyze differences in immigrant students' test scores by country of origin. The international PISA samples are plagued by small immigrant samples and inadequate country-of-origin information. We partly overcome these challenges by combining the samples from three Danish PISA studies with an above-average percentage of immigrants and by linking information on country of origin from Danish administrative registers. In addition, we use data on home background and individual migration histories linked from administrative registers.

We find that differences in socioeconomic characteristics can explain about 40-50% of the test score gap relative to native Danes for Turkey, Lebanon and former Yugoslavia, and some more for students from Pakistan (65%). However, even adjusted gaps remain sizeable and statistically significant. The adjusted gap is largest for students from Lebanon (0.80 SD), somewhat smaller for students from Turkey and former Yugoslavia and Afghanistan (about 0.55 SD), and smallest for Pakistan (about 0.25 SD). Thus, while the results indicate that a major portion of the test score gaps can be attributed to less favourable socioeconomic background factors of immigrant students, educational achievement of young immigrants is poorer than that of native Danish youngsters even after conditioning on the socioeconomic status of their family.

Subsample regressions suggest that while adjusted gaps are smaller for the second generation than for the first generation for most countries of origin, gaps are still large even in the second generation for students originating from Lebanon, former Yugoslavia and Turkey. For all source countries, students who mainly speak Danish at home do better compared to those who speak the heritage language at home – for Danish-speaking families from former Yugoslavia and Pakistan, the test score gap even reduces to zero. On the other hand, for students from Turkey the differences are small.

Further analyses show that differences in schools explain only little of the test score gap, while suggestive evidence on differences in cultural differences concerning attitudes and expectations towards family and working life can explain part of the remaining gap. For Pakistanis, this even explains the entire remaining gap – so, cultural differences seem to matter. Yet, as mentioned above, we cannot be sure that these results are not at least partly driven by mere correlation. We conclude by suggesting further possible sources of the test score gap (ethnic capital in the source country and among compatriots in Denmark, consanguineous marriage), but a rigorous assessment of their relationship to test score gaps must be deferred to future work.

Appendix Table A1: Selected means of variables in the three PISA datasets.

Variable	PISA 2000 Obs	PISA 2000 Mean	PISA KK Obs	PISA KK Mean	PISA E Obs	PISA E Mean
Non-Western immigrant	3730	0,049	1898	0,274	3849	0,309
No. Immigs		182		521		1189
First generation (non-Western) immigrant	3730	0,032	1898	0,110	3849	0,137
Second generation (non-Western) immigrant	3730	0,016	1898	0,165	3849	0,172
Speaks Danish at home	3710	0,937	1786	0,764	3482	0,777
Father's years of schooling	3674	11,919	1835	11,754	3762	11,565
Mother's years of schooling	3709	11,729	1897	11,564	3833	11,195
Lives with both parents	3675	0,689	1869	0,663	3763	0,688
Number of siblings	3730	0,791	1898	1,202	3849	1,101
Highest Occupational Level of Parents (HISEI)	3476	49,625	1708	50,836	.	.
Cultural communication	3660	0,106	.	.	3724	0,220
Social communication	3664	0,204	.	.	3766	0,239
Cultural possessions	3679	-0,130	.	.	3758	-0,227
Home educational resources	3704	-0,217	.	.	3789	-1,288
More than 250 books in home	3611	0,299	1820	0,287	3167	0,260

Cultural communication: "In general, how often do your parents: (1-5; never or hardly ever - several times a week)"

Discuss political or social issues with you?	.	.	1756	3,036	.	.
Discuss books, films or television programmes with you?	.	.	1756	3,470	.	.
Listen to classical music with you?	.	.	1756	1,613	.	.

Social communication "In general, how often do your parents: (1-5; never or hardly ever - several times a week)"

Discuss how well you are doing at school?	.	.	1756	4,217	.	.
Eat "the main meal" with you around a table?	.	.	1756	4,736	.	.
Spend time just talking to you?	.	.	1756	4,560	.	.

Cultural possessions: "In your home, do you have: (1=yes)"

Classical literature	.	.	1733	1,535	.	.
Books of poetry	.	.	1733	1,530	.	.
Works of art	.	.	1733	1,337	.	.

Home educational resources: "In your home, do you have:"

A dictionary (1=yes)	.	.	1733	1,032	.	.
A quiet place to study (1=yes)	.	.	1733	1,176	.	.
A desk for study (1=yes)	.	.	1733	1,084	.	.
Text books (1=yes)	.	.	1733	1,492	.	.
How many calculators do you have in your home?						
(1-4; none - three or more)	.	.	1841	3,647	.	.
Years since arrival	.	.	.	.	3849	1,465
Mother's years of work experience in Denmark	.	.	.	.	3320	12,228
Father's years of work experience in Denmark	.	.	.	.	3307	15,788
Mother self-employed	.	.	.	.	3744	0,030
Mother high job position	.	.	.	.	3744	0,104
Mother medium/low job position	.	.	.	.	3744	0,567
Mother not working	.	.	.	.	3744	0,299
Father self-employed	.	.	.	.	3320	0,075
Father high job position	.	.	.	.	3320	0,168
Father medium/low job position	.	.	.	.	3320	0,525
Father not working	.	.	.	.	3320	0,231
Household income (1,000 DKK)	.	.	.	.	2789	456

Appendix Table A2. Full Sample Results.

	Coef.	Robust Std. Err	P>|t|	Coef.	Robust Std. Err	P>|t|	Coef.	Robust Std. Err	P>|t|	Without PISA 2000 data Coef.	Robust Std. Err	P>|t|
Turkey	108,289	5,380	0,000	-59,834	5,621	0,000	-56,140	5,136	0,000	-56,735	5,675	0,000
Lebanon	131,336	8,500	0,000	-85,233	9,308	0,000	-78,953	9,140	0,000	-80,288	9,900	0,000
F. Yugoslavia	-92,782	6,999	0,000	-63,556	6,859	0,000	-55,402	6,598	0,000	-52,394	7,575	0,000
Pakistan	-75,764	8,321	0,000	-31,464	8,222	0,000	-27,459	8,014	0,001	-25,262	8,344	0,003
Female				26,504	1,971	0,000	21,180	1,914	0,000	21,138	2,529	0,000
Father: years of schooling				3,723	0,320	0,000	2,640	0,309	0,000	2,441	0,378	0,000
Mother: years of schooling				3,485	0,329	0,000	2,407	0,312	0,000	2,062	0,389	0,000
Lived with both parents				4,105	2,296	0,075	-0,284	2,189	0,897	-5,613	3,036	0,066
No. siblings				-0,433	1,123	0,700	0,447	1,054	0,672	-0,927	1,328	0,486
Occupational status (index)				1,007	0,087	0,000	0,635	0,080	0,000	0,715	0,128	0,000
Cultural communication							18,370	1,412	0,000	18,258	2,253	0,000
Social communication							2,070	1,416	0,145	0,016	2,055	0,994
Cultural posessions							2,936	1,233	0,018	3,463	1,666	0,039
Home educational resources							5,101	1,096	0,000	6,368	1,511	0,000
No. books at home							14,067	2,473	0,000	13,519	3,384	0,000
Father:												
Self-employed				Reference			Reference			Reference		
High occup. status				26,122	8,572	0,002	22,867	7,958	0,004	23,816	8,036	0,003
Middle/low occup. status				11,750	7,485	0,117	16,093	7,374	0,030	16,053	7,419	0,032
Not working				11,646	7,503	0,121	13,100	7,118	0,066	12,427	7,133	0,083
Mother:												
Self-employed				Reference			Reference			Reference		
High occup. status				25,103	10,004	0,012	19,156	9,527	0,045	20,647	9,531	0,031
Middle/low occup. status				0,232	8,702	0,979	4,350	8,300	0,600	4,990	8,357	0,551
Not working				-8,948	9,997	0,371	-5,551	9,675	0,566	-5,528	9,758	0,572
Mother: years of labour market experience				-0,078	0,272	0,774	-0,092	0,271	0,734	-0,122	0,278	0,661
Father: years of labour market experience				21,928	23,044	0,342	0,199	0,265	0,454	0,160	0,269	0,553
Household income/1000				0,015	0,007	0,026	0,010	0,006	0,140	0,012	0,007	0,082
Constant	499,558	2,000	0,000	360,660	15,190	0,000	442,520	24,612	0,000	447,882	31,901	0,000
Obs	9477			9477			9477			5747		
R-sq	0,138			0,247			0,310			0,331		

Note: Missing value flags and single items of composites are included in all regressions.

References

Abu-Rabia, S. and L. Maroun (2005): The effect of consanguineous marriage on reading disability in the Arab community. *Dyslexia*, Volume 11, Issue 1, Pages 1–21.

Adsera, A. and B. R. Chiswick (2007): Are there gender and country of origin differences in immigrant labor market outcomes across European destinations? *Journal of Population Economics*, 20(3): 495-526.

Banerjee, B. and L. Bandyopadhyay (2005): Gender differences in nutritional status. *Indian pediatrics*. 42:400.

Bauer, P. and R. T. Riphahn (2007): Heterogeneity in the intergenerational transmission of educational attainment: evidence from Switzerland on natives and second-generation immigrants. *Journal of Population Economics*, 20(1):121-148.

Bittles, A. H. (2008): Map downloaded from: http://www.consang.net/index.php/Global_prevalence (Oct 15, 2008)

Blau, F. D., L. M. Kahn, and K.L. Papps, (2008): Gender, Source Country Characteristics and Labor Market Assimilation Among Immigrants, 1980-2000. *NBER WP* 14387.

Böcker, A. (1994): Chain migration over legally closed borders: Settled immigrants as bridgeheads and gatekeepers. *Netherlands Journal of Social Science*. 30(2): 87-106.

Buchinsky, M. (1998): Recent advances in quantile regression models: a practical guideline for empirical research. *Journal of Human Resources* 33(1): 88-126.

Celikaksoy, A., P. Jensen, and N. Smith, (2007): *Marital behaviour and the educational attainment of young Danish immigrants*. Manuscript.

Chiswick, B. R. and N. DebBurman (2004): Educational Attainment: Analysis by Immigrant Generation. *Economics of Education Review*, 23(4), August 2004, pp. 361-379.

Chiswick, B. R., A.T. Le, and P.W. Miller, (2006): How Immigrants Fare Across the Earnings Distribution: International Analyses, *Industrial and Labor Relations Review*, 2008, 61 (3), 353-373.

Corry P.C. (2002): Intellectual disability and cerebral palsy in a UK community. Community Genetics, 5: 201–4.

Cortes, K. E. (2004): Are refugees different from economic immigrants? Some empirical evidence on the heterogeneity of immigrant groups in the United States. *IZA Discussion Paper* No. 1063.

Entorf, H. and N. Minoiu, (2005): What a difference immigration policy makes: A comparison of PISA scores in Europe and traditional countries of immigration. *German Economic Review* 6(3), 355-376.

Jakobsen, V. and N. Smith (2003): The Educational Attainment of the Children of the Danish Guest Worker Immigrants. *IZA Discussion Paper* No. 749/SFI Working Paper 3:2003.

Kandamuthan, M. (1997): The effect of consanguineous marriage on the disability of their children. *Journal of Clinical Epidemiology*, 50(1):13S-13S(1).

Kristen, C. and N. Granato, (2007): The educational attainment of the second generation in Germany. *Ethnicities*, Vol. 7, No. 3, 343-366.

McEwan, P. J. (2008): Can schools reduce the indigenous test score gap? Evidence from Chile. *Journal of Development Studies*, forthcoming.

Nielsen, H. S., M. Rosholm, N. Smith, and L. Husted (2003): Intergenerational transmission and the school-to-work transition for second generation immigrants. *Journal of Population Economics*, 16:755-786.

Nielsen, H. S., N. Smith, and A. Celikaksoy (2007). The Effect of Marriage on Education of Immigrants: Evidence from a Policy Reform Restricting Spouse Import. *IZA Discussion Paper* No. 2899.

Pedersen, S. (1999): Migration to and from Denmark during the period 1960-97. In: *Immigration to Denmark*, Coleman & Wadensjö, eds. (1999).

Rangvid, B.S. (2007): Sources of immigrants' underachievement: Results from PISA-Copenhagen. *Education Economics:* 15(3), 293-326.

Riphahn, R. T. (2003): Cohort effects in the educational attainment of second generation immigrants in Germany. *Journal of Population Economics*, 16:711-737.

Rooth, D.-O. and J. Ekberg, (2003): Unemployment and earnings for second generation immigrants – ethnic background and parent composition. Journal of *Population Economics* 16: 787-814.

Schnepf, S. V. (2007): Immigrants' educational disadvantage: an examination across ten countries and three surveys. *Journal of Population Economics*, 20:527-545.

Schoenbaum, M., T. Tulchinsky, and H. Abed, (1995): Gender differences in nutritional status and feeding patterns among infants in the Gaza Strip. *American journal of public health.* 85(7): 965-969.

Surén, P., A. Grjibovski, and C. Stoltenberg, (2007): Inngifte i Norge: Omfang og medisinske konsekvenser. *Folkehelseinstitut*, rapport 2007:2.

Van Ours, J. C. and J. Veenman, (2003): The educational attainment of second-generation immigrants in The Netherlands. *Journal of Population Economics*, 16:739-753.

Zere, E. and D. McIntyre, (2003): Inequities in under-five child malnutrition in South Africa. *Int J Equity Health*. 2:7.

Publications in English from the Rockwool Foundation Research Unit

Time and Consumption
Edited by Gunnar Viby Mogensen. With contributions by Søren Brodersen, Thomas Gelting, Niels Buus Kristensen, Eszter Körmendi, Lisbeth Pedersen, Benedicte Madsen. Niels Ploug, Erik Ib Schmidt, Rewal Schmidt Sørensen, and Gunnar Viby Mogensen (Statistics Denmark, Copenhagen. 1990)

Danes and Their Politicians
By Gunnar Viby Mogensen (Aarhus University Press. 1993)

Solidarity or Egoism?
By Douglas A. Hibbs (Aarhus University Press. 1993)

Welfare and Work Incentives. A North European Perspective
Edited by A.B. Atkinson and Gunnar Viby Mogensen. With Contributions by A.B. Atkinson, Richard Blundell, Björn Gustafsson, Anders Klevmarken, Peder J. Pedersen, and Klaus Zimmermann (Oxford University Press. 1993)

Unemployment and Flexibility on the Danish Labour Market
By Gunnar Viby Mogensen (Statistics Denmark, Copenhagen. 1994)

On the Measurement of a Welfare Indicator for Denmark 1970-1990
By Peter Rørmose Jensen and Elisabeth Møllgaard (Statistics Denmark, Copenhagen. 1995)

The Shadow Economy in Denmark 1994. Measurement and Results
By Gunnar Viby Mogensen, Hans Kurt Kvist, Eszter Körmendi, and Søren Pedersen (Statistics Denmark, Copenhagen. 1995)

Work Incentives in the Danish Welfare State: New Empirical Evidence
Edited by Gunnar Viby Mogensen. With contributions by Søren Brodersen, Lisbeth Pedersen, Peder J. Pedersen, Søren Pedersen, and Nina Smith (Aarhus University Press. 1995)

Actual and Potential Recipients of Welfare Benefits with a Focus on Housing Benefits, 1987-1992
By Hans Hansen and Marie Louise Hultin (Statistics Denmark, Copenhagen. 1997)

The Shadow Economy in Western Europe. Measurement and Results for Selected Countries
By Søren Pedersen. With contributions by Esben Dalgaard and Gunnar Viby Mogensen (Statistics Denmark, Copenhagen. 1998)

Immigration to Denmark. International and National Perspectives
By David Coleman and Eskil Wadensjö. With contributions by Bent Jensen and Søren Pedersen (Aarhus University Press. 1999)

Nature as a Political Issue in the Classical Industrial Society: The Environmental Debate in the Danish Press from the 1870s to the 1970s
By Bent Jensen (Statistics Denmark, Copenhagen. 2000)

Foreigners in the Danish newspaper debate from the 1870s to the 1990s
By Bent Jensen (Statistics Denmark, Copenhagen. 2001)

The integration of non-Western immigrants in a Scandinavian labour market: The Danish experience
By Marie Louise Schultz-Nielsen. With contributions by Olaf Ingerslev, Claus Larsen, Gunnar Viby Mogensen, Niels-Kenneth Nielsen, Søren Pedersen, and Eskil Wadensjö (Statistics Denmark, Copenhagen. 2001)

Immigration and the public sector in Denmark
By Eskil Wadensjö and Helena Orrje (Aarhus University Press. 2002)

Social security in Denmark and Germany – with a focus on access conditions for refugees and immigrants. A comparative study
By Hans Hansen, Helle Cwarzko Jensen, Claus Larsen, and Niels-Kenneth Nielsen (Statistics Denmark, Copenhagen. 2002)

The Shadow Economy in Germany, Great Britain, and Scandinavia. A Measurement Based on Questionnaire Surveys
By Søren Pedersen (Statistics Denmark, Copenhagen. 2003)

Do-it-yourself work in North-Western Europe. Maintenance and improvement of homes
By Søren Brodersen (Statistics Denmark, Copenhagen. 2003)

Migrants, Work, and the Welfare State
Edited by Torben Tranæs and Klaus F. Zimmermann. With contributions by Thomas Bauer, Amelie Constant, Horst Entorf, Christer Gerdes, Claus Larsen, Poul Chr. Matthiessen, Niels-Kenneth Nielsen, Marie Louise Schultz-Nielsen, and Eskil Wadensjö (University Press of Southern Denmark. 2004)

Black Activities in Germany in 2001 and in 2004. A Comparison Based on Survey Data
By Lars P. Feld and Claus Larsen (Statistics Denmark, Copenhagen. 2005)

From Asylum Seeker to Refugee to Family Reunification. Welfare Payments in These Situations in Various Western Countries
By Hans Hansen (Statistics Denmark, Copenhagen. 2006)

A Comparison of Welfare Payments to Asylum Seekers, Refugees, and Reunified Families. In Selected European Countries and in Canada
By Torben Tranæs, Bent Jensen, and Mark Gervasini Nielsen (Statistics Denmark, Copenhagen. 2006)

Employment Effects of Reducing Welfare to Refugees
By Duy T. Huynh, Marie Louise Schultz-Nielsen, and Torben Tranæs (The Rockwool Foundation Research Unit. 2007)

Determination of Net Transfers for Immigrants in Germany
By Christer Gerdes (The Rockwool Foundation Research Unit. 2007)

What happens to the Employment of Native Co-Workers when Immigrants are Hired?
By Nikolaj Malchow-Møller, Jakob Roland Munch, and Jan Rose Skaksen (The Rockwool Foundation Research Unit. 2007)

Immigrants at the Workplace and the Wages of Native Workers
By Nikolaj Malchow-Møller, Jakob Roland Munch, and Jan Rose Skaksen (The Rockwool Foundation Research Unit. 2007)

Crime and Partnerships
By Michael Svarer (University Press of Southern Denmark, The Rockwool Foundation Research Unit. 2008)

Immigrant and Native Children's Cognitive Outcomes and the Effect of Ethnic Concentration in Danish Schools
By Peter Jensen and Astrid Würtz Rasmussen (University Press of Southern Denmark, The Rockwool Foundation Research Unit. 2008)

The Unemployed in the Danish Newspaper Debate from the 1840s to the 1990s
By Bent Jensen (University Press of Southern Denmark, The Rockwool Foundation Research Unit. 2008)

Source Country Differences in Test Score Gaps: Evidence from Denmark
By Beatrice Schindler Rangvid (University Press of Southern Denmark, The Rockwool Foundation Research Unit. 2008)

The Rockwool Foundation Research Unit on the Internet

Completely updated information, e.g. about the latest projects of the Research Unit, can be found on the Internet on the home page of the Research Unit at the address:

www.rff.dk

The home page includes in a Danish and an English version:

- a commented survey of publications stating distributors of the books of the Research Unit

- survey of research projects

- information about the organization and staff of the Research Unit

- information about data base and choice of method and

- newsletters from the Research Unit

Printed newsletters from the Rockwool Foundation Research Unit can also be ordered free of charge on telephone +45 39 17 38 32.